D0586187

STUDIES IN ECONOMIC GROWTH, NO. I

General Editor : V. K. R. V. RAO

THE ROLE OF SMALL ENTERPRISES IN
INDIAN ECONOMIC DEVELOPMENT

INSTITUTE OF ECONOMIC GROWTH

Studies in Economic Growth

1. *The Role of Small Enterprises in Indian Economic Development* by P. N. Dhar and H. F. Lydall

2. *Indian Tax Structure and Economic Development* by G. S. Sahota

INSTITUTE OF ECONOMIC GROWTH

DELHI

The Role of
Small Enterprises in
Indian Economic Development

P. N. Dhar
Institute of Economic Growth, Delhi

and

H. F. Lydall
Massachusetts Institute of Technology

ASIA PUBLISHING HOUSE
BOMBAY - CALCUTTA - NEW DELHI - MADRAS
LONDON - NEW YORK

Printed in India

by Michael Andrades at The Bombay Chronicle Press, Horniman
Circle, Bombay 1 and Published by P. S. Jayasinghe, Asia Publishing
House, Bombay 1.

PREFACE

As part of its research programme, the Institute of Economic Growth proposes to bring out a series of monographs entitled *Studies in Economic Growth* setting out some of the results of the research work of its staff and scholars. These monographs will mainly concentrate on some of the major problems concerning economic growth in India.

This monograph is a result of a programme of collaboration in research between this Institute, and the M.I.T. Centre for International Studies, Cambridge, Massachusetts. It was undertaken jointly by Mr. P. N. Dhar, Fellow of the Institute, and Mr. H. F. Lydall, who worked in the Institute as a Visiting Fellow on behalf of the M.I.T. Centre for a period of six months. It is a study of the role of small enterprises in India's economic growth based on an analysis of first principles and an examination of the actual data available on the working of small industries during recent years in this country. It contains a special examination of the working of industrial estates as an instrument for the promotion of small industries and makes suggestions for a modification of current official policy on the subject, both based on data specially collected from many industrial estates operating in the country, and supplemented by personal visits to selected ones among them.

In placing this monograph before the general public, the Institute hopes that a more rational and objective discussion will follow on the role of small industries in Indian economic development and this, in turn, will lead to the formulation and adoption of policy regarding small industries that will be more suited to growth and efficient expansion than perhaps is the case with the current official thinking on the subject.

Institute of Economic Growth,   V. K. R. V. RAO
Delhi.   Director
June 1961.

EDITOR'S INTRODUCTION

In their interesting study which forms the subject of this monograph the authors draw a sharp distinction between what may be called traditional small industries and modern small industries and suggest that many of the arguments that are advanced in support of small industries in both official and non-official circles really relate to the former and do not have much relevance for the latter. They identify the former with labour-intensive and largely rural or village industries using traditional methods (lacking power and machinery) for making traditional products, while the latter are largely urban industries, using both power and machinery, and techniques of production more or less similar to those employed by the so-called large industries, and manufacturing modern products of more or less the same type as those produced by the large industries. The authors confine their attention in this study to the latter type of small industries, viz., those which employ modern methods for manufacturing modern products using both power and machinery, are located in urban centres, and cater to markets and draw their raw materials and other components from centres distant from the place of manufacture. As illustration of the type of small industries they have in mind may be mentioned metal utensils, bicycle parts, sewing machines, machine tools, razor blades, radio sets, electric motors, polythene bags, spectacle frames and a wide variety of other modern products.

After examining in some detail the arguments usually advanced in support of small industries, viz., that they are labour-intensive, lead to decentralisation in the sense of being more easily located in villages or small towns, promote equality or democracy, and help to draw out latent scarce resources, especially of entrepreneurship and capital, they come to the conclusion that these arguments are not particularly valid as far as the modern type of small industries is concerned. In fact, in their opinion, these small factories (employing between 10 and 49 persons) are actually capital-intensive, i.e., use more capital per unit of output than the large factories, more especially when one takes into account the virtual impossibility of operating these small proprietorial concerns on a double or triple shift basis; they pay lower wages and possibly also smaller levels of remuneration to their entrepreneurs, and far from being decentralised, are almost entirely located in towns and for the most part in the large cities. They conclude that, apart from political arguments, which they consider to be outside their province, the only important argument in favour of small enterprises is that they spread the total income generated more widely over the population. As against this, they point out that this may lead to a smaller income in the future or "the price of more (lower paid) jobs now may be fewer 'decent jobs' in the future." The authors draw attention to the fact that in other countries, the medium sized firm (with say 50-499 employees) plays a larger role, and appropriately so, as they come nearer to the optimum size, especially in the higher manufacturing trades, and conclude:

"The main lesson of our study of this problem is that there is need for more firms of a medium size, because the capital-intensive techniques which characterise modern small enterprises can, in many cases, be fully productive only if they are worked on a larger scale than at present. Any positive measures that can be taken to promote the *growth* of small firms into efficient medium-sized firms will, therefore, be of great advantage to the economy."

Proceeding on the basis of this conclusion, the authors express the view that as far as modern small industrial enterprises are concerned — their study is confined to this sector of small industries — there is no good case for giving them preferential treatment. They agree that there is a good case for having a special programme of assistance to small industries : but this programme should take the form of assistance for removing their disabilities rather than of giving them special favours such as preferences. subsidies, reserved markets and the like. Thus, they call for a reorientation in the official policy regarding small scale industrial units of the modern type. What these enterprises require is the removal of their disabilities, not the conferment of a positive advantage. Thus, the authors would favour the giving of technical advice but, beyond a certain point, it should be charged for. They would favour the setting up of institutional channels to give small enterprises easier access to capital, but not a subsidised price. They would help them to establish marketing contacts, but not take over the responsibility for selling their products. They would favour the setting up of industrial estates for giving them factory premises, but not at heavily subsidised rents. In fine, they would like to stimulate the growth of the small industrial units into more efficient and possibly larger-sized units rather than keep them stagnant and uneconomic by just protecting them.

The chapter on "The Industrial Estates Programme" merits special attention on the part of the reader. In effect, the conclusion that the authors reach is that industrial estates do not constitute an effective instrument either for industrialising rural areas or for generally promoting industrialisation irrespective of the economic and entrepreneurial background against which these estates are located. For pioneering industrialisation in areas which at the moment lack industries, the authors would pin their faith on the large industries. In their view, small industry is a follower rather than a pioneer and it is large industry that will create external economies of agglomeration as well as provide potential small entrepreneurs from among the ranks of its skilled workers. They are in favour of continuing the programme of industrial estates provided they are located in areas where industrialisation has already made some headway and a supply of entrepreneurial skills already exist, costs of construction are brought down to the minimum, suitable rents are charged, and the estates are used not so much for creating larger employment opportunities as for serving as nursery beds in which efficient small entrepreneurs can grow. As I read their conclusions, I believe they regard industrial estates more as centres of favourable opportunities where small industrial enterprises can grow in efficiency and size and then graduate by getting out into the larger world for securing opportunities for larger growth, leaving other small industrial units to occupy the places vacated by them in the industrial estates and to grow and then leave, in turn to be replaced by still other small industrial units. That is why they would treat industrial estates as nursery beds for the growth of small units rather than as permanent houses for the many and growing number of small industrial enterprises. This would involve a reorientation in the present policy regarding industrial estates and, if accepted, may make for a reduction in the vast expansion programme contemplated in the Third Plan in the number and location of new industrial estates.

The authors then subject to a critical analysis the other items in the official programme for assisting small enterprises under the six heads of technical, financial and marketing assistance, training of workers, supply of raw materials and power, and advice on the starting of new enterprises. On the whole, there is commendation for the policies followed by Government in these fields, except in so far as assistance takes the form of special privileges, preferences, quotas, reservations, and the like. The authors do not like crutches and are opposed to spoon-feeding. They want the removal of disabilities and the promotion of competition rather than an ideological fervour in favour of small enterprises as such. Thus, they would confine marketing assistance to be limited to measures designed to spread information and perfect the market rather than provide a guaranteed or protected market, as, in their opinion, the latter is less likely to stimulate enterprise than to spread stagnation by the elimination of the spur of competition. It is worth while quoting the conclusion with which they end this fascinating study.

"The major lesson that can be drawn from this study is the importance of concentrating on the promotion of *efficiency* and *growth* rather than on the creation of new small firms for their own sake. We believe that there is an important role for small enterprises to play in Indian economic development but that the main encouragement should be given to the most efficient and promising small firms and that all must learn to stand on their own feet."

The brief account given above should show the importance of this study for all who are interested in a rational and efficient acceleration of India's industrial growth. All may not agree with either their analysis or their conclusions, but there is no denying the amount of careful thought and meticulous scholarship that have gone into this study nor can one help admiring the courage shown by the authors in their refusal to be inhibited by current orthodoxy or official thinking.

ACKNOWLEDGEMENTS

IT would not have been possible to have carried out this study without the assistance of a large number of officials of the Government, both in Delhi and in the States. To all of them we express our gratitude for the time and efforts they devoted to our inquiry. Needless to say, none of them should be held responsible for anything that we have said or failed to say. We trust that, even where they disagree with our conclusions, they will find our arguments provocative of thought.

Amongst those who should particularly be mentioned are: at the Centre, Sir V. T. Krishnamachari, Deputy-Chairman of the Planning Commission, Mr. Tarlok Singh, Mr. Pitambar Pant and Dr. D. K. Malhotra (also of the Planning Commission), Dr. P. C. Alexander (of the Ministry of Commerce and Industry), Dr. S. L. Sharma and Mr. M. M. Bhatnagar (of the Small Scale Industries Organisation); and in the States, Dr. J. N. Thadani, Mr. Anil De, Mr. T. K. Palaniappan, Mr. S. V. Raghavan, Dr. P. V. Nair, Mr. K. K. Raja, Mr. A. Sambamoorthy and Mr V. V. Apte.

We are particularly indebted to the various States officers who helped to complete our schedules of inquiry about the industrial estates and the factories working in them.

Mr. J. N. Sharma, of the Institute of Economic Growth, was responsible for collecting data from the factories in Okhla industrial estate and assisted with tabulation and computing and in other ways. Mr. N. K. Goil, Librarian of the Institute, prepared the index. Mr. Mafooz Ahmed, of the Indian Statistical Institute, also helped with some of the computations.

P.N.D.
H.F.L.

CONTENTS

CONTENTS

INTRODUCTION

THE promotion of small-scale industries has been widely recommended as one of the most appropriate means of developing industry in over-populated, backward countries. Japan is usually held up as the great example of what can be done in this way; and now, even communist China is said to be following a similar path, at least in the rural areas. In no country, however, has the doctrine of small industry received such strong official support as in India. There are a number of reasons for this. The most important is the legacy of Gandhian teaching. In addition, the very wide distribution of *existing* small industry in India, the great pressure of population, and the shortage of capital have all tended to direct attention towards the small-scale sector as a possible means of increasing output and employment in Indian industry for at least the next few decades.

Government interest in small industries began in a fairly small way. In the First Five Year Plan, only Rs. 34 crores was spent on all village and small industries, of which more than two-thirds was on khadi and handloom. But it was during the First Plan that a number of special boards were set up to take responsibility for administering Government programmes for small industries. These covered handloom, khadi and village industries, handicrafts, sericulture, coir and "small-scale" industries. Thus, by the end of the First Plan, the stage was set for a considerable expansion of effort in this field. The total amount allocated for village and small industries in the Second Plan (as revised) was Rs. 177 crores. Out of this, khadi and handloom were still to receive about half; but there was a large increase in the allocation to "small-scale industries" — which means, broadly, all the small manufacturing enterprises not covered by the specialised industry boards. The amount provided for this group increased from less than Rs. 5 crores (actually spent) in the First Plan, to Rs. 55 crores in the Second. (The latter figure includes the allocation for industrial estates.) According to the Draft Outline of the Third Five Year Plan, the total allocation for villages and small industries in the Third Plan will rise to Rs. 250 crores, of which the share of "small-scale industries" will be Rs. 107 crores. Thus, the share of "small-scale" industries will go up from about 30 per cent in the Second Plan, to about 43 per cent in the Third Plan.

It is only natural that the increase in expenditure on small industries should have been accompanied by an increasing urge, both within and outside the Government, to review the progress of the work and to suggest further lines of advance. In 1954, a special survey was undertaken by an international planning team sponsored by the Ford Foundation; in 1959, a further study was made by a Japanese delegation; and various other working groups on evaluation, and on future planning, have been sponsored by the Government from time to time. But most of these studies have had a very "practical" bias; they have been concerned more with the working out of the programme than with the assumptions underlying it.

The purpose of this paper is to attempt to make a contribution towards a more fundamental consideration of the aims of small industry promotion work. In the first section that follows we shall give an outline of the present structure of manufacturing industry in India. In the next, we shall consider critically the main arguments that have been put forward for giving special assistance to small industries and, in the light of that discussion, suggest the principles on which small industry policy in India should be based. The next section will be devoted to a special study of industrial estates, the establishment of which has become one of the major instruments of small industry policy in India. And finally, we shall review the operation of other main programmes of assistance to small industries, with a view to suggesting the most appropriate lines of future development.

P.N.D.

H.F.L.

CHAPTER I

THE STRUCTURE OF MANUFACTURING INDUSTRY IN INDIA

BEFORE we approach some of the wider questions of small industry policy it is necessary to try to form a clear picture of the character and dimensions of existing small industry in India. Most discussions of small industry policy reflect a state of considerable confusion about what is meant by "small industries" in the Indian context.

It should, of course, be obvious that the phrase "small industry" is a misnomer. The problem to be discussed is not the development of small *industries* but of small *enterprises*. (The handloom industry — which is a pre-eminent example of a "small industry" — employs at least 3 million people and supplies nearly a third of the total Indian consumption of cotton textiles.) How the adjective "small" (or "small-scale") became attached to the word "industry" rather than to the word "enterprise" (or "unit", "firm", "factory", etc.) is itself an instructive story; for, it reveals some of the mistaken assumptions of those involved in the formulation of policy in this field.

Indian small-scale enterprises can be divided, broadly, into two main types. First, there are the traditional cottage enterprises, or, as they are correctly called, cottage *industries*. The hallmark of these enterprises is that they use *traditional methods* to make *traditional products*. It is the latter characteristic which entitles them, as a group, to be referred to as an "industry". The products of handlooms, for example, are not only made by a traditional technique but they bear on themselves the marks of that technique: they are handloom *cloth*. The same applies to hand-pounded rice, gur, and other traditional products. A number of other characteristics arise out of the technical nature of traditional industries; most of the units operating in these industries are located in *villages*; they are almost entirely *household* enterprises (employing little or no hired labour); most of them derive their raw materials from *local sources*; and they sell most of their products in *local*

1

markets.[1] They are, in sum, small-scale, rural, localised and technically backward.

The second main type of small-scale enterprise is entirely different. These are *modern* small firms, employing modern techniques to produce modern products. A great many such firms are in the engineering and chemical industries. They produce such things as metal utensils, bicycle parts, sewing machines, machine tools, razor blades, radio sets, electric motors, polythene bags, spectacle frames and a wide variety of other modern products. These firms, by their nature, are generally located in *towns* rather than in villages (in fact, they cluster particularly in the large cities); they are, generally, not purely household enterprises but employ mainly *hired labour*; they use raw materials (such as steel and chemicals) which often come from *long distances* (either from the few Indian plants or from overseas); and they sell their products *very widely*, not merely in the nearest town, but over one or more States, and even in some cases in export markets. It is obvious that enterprises of this type cannot sensibly be described as small "industries", since they belong to wider industries embracing both medium and large-scale firms. The use of the term "small industry" to cover this type of enterprise only causes confusion.

It is arguable that one should allow for the existence of a third main type of small enterprise: those that are *intermediate* between the *traditional* and the *modern*. Intermediate enterprises might be defined as those that use more or less *traditional techniques* to produce more or less *modern products*. For example, western style shoes can be made by hand instead of by machine; and the same applies to furniture, brushes, bricks, candles, soap, matches and other products. But, on closer analysis, it appears that these firms are using not so much "traditional" techniques (the products themselves are modern) as labour-intensive capital-saving techniques. It seems preferable, therefore, to include most of these cases under the "modern" heading, with the qualification that they are using techniques which are not fully "modern", in the sense that they are largely unmechanised. In any case, by the nature of their products, these firms are necessarily in sharp competition

---

[1] Exception to this are some urban handicrafts, like Kashmir shawls, Benares brocade and Mirzapur carpets, which supply both national and international markets.

with more mechanised firms in the same industry.

How big are these two main types of small "industry"? Some broad indications can be obtained from data collected by the National Sample Survey, which are reproduced in Tables 1 and 2. Table 1 shows the estimated number of persons gainfully occupied in manufacturing, classified by type of enterprise and by urban or rural residence.[2] The classification of enterprises given in the table is a condensation of the classification used in the survey. It will be noted that the first two classes fall below the usual Factory Act limits, the third class falls between the Factory Act limits and the limits at which factories become "large units" under the Industries (Development and Regulation) Act, 1951; and the fourth class includes all "large-scale" units as that term is normally applied in India.

TABLE 1

DISTRIBUTION OF EMPLOYMENT BY TYPE OF ENTERPRISE
AND URBAN OR RURAL RESIDENCE, 1955

(thousands)

Type of enterprise	Rural	Urban	Total
1. Employing less than 10 with power, or 20 without, using mainly household labour	8,068	2,821	10,889
2. Employing less than 10 with power, or 20 without, using mainly hired labour	833	897	1,730
3. Employing 10-49 with power, or 20-99 without	197	298	495
4. Employing 50 or more with power, or 100 or more without	1,438	1,650	3,088
TOTAL	10,536	5,666	16,202

SOURCE: Special tabulation made for the Perspective Planning Division of the Planning Commission from employment data collected in the Ninth Round of the National Sample Survey, May-November 1955.

[2] Each person in the interviewed households—of which there were about 25,000 altogether—was asked for his "usual industrial status", which means the activity which took up most of his time during the previous year. Gainfully occupied people (described here as "employed" persons), were also asked about the size and type of enterprise in which they were engaged (presumably, again, for the majority of their time in the previous year).

According to the National Sample Survey, the total number of persons employed in manufacturing in India, in 1955, was 16.2 million. This figure includes everyone who said that he was working in manufacturing for most of his time; and it may well include a large number of workers in household enterprises who spent more of their time on "manufacturing" than on any other identifiable activity. The figure is somewhat larger than one would expect on the basis of the estimate from the 1951 Census, which was of the order of 13 million. (Manufacturing employment could not possibly have increased by 3 million in four years.) But it seems likely that the Census excluded many unpaid family workers from its class of "earning dependents". This discrepancy is a symptom of the very real difficulty of classifying unpaid household workers into categories derived from a monetised economy.

We can see from Table 1 that, of the total of 16.2 million persons engaged in "manufacturing", about half were employed in rural household enterprises; and a further 2.8 million were in urban household enterprises, making nearly 11 million altogether in household, cottage, almost entirely *traditional* industry. In the non-household group below the Factory Act limits there were a further 1.7 million persons, of which (as can be seen in Table 2) the majority were also engaged in traditional industry. The next group—employing 10-49 with power or 20-99 without—is small (only about half a million) but, it has, interestingly enough, the largest proportion of urban employees; and, as can be seen from Table 2, it includes a substantial proportion of workers engaged in the more modern types of industry. Finally, "large-scale" enterprises employ about 3 million persons. It is remarkable to find that nearly half of these are living in rural areas; and this suggests that large-scale enterprise is less restricted in its choice of location than is often believed. (Part of the explanation may also be that workers *living* in rural areas *work* in large-scale enterprises which themselves are located in towns.)

The object of Table 2 is to throw some light on the relation between type of product and size of enterprise. The industries have been grouped very roughly into "mainly traditional" products (such as foodstuffs, tobacco, leather and wood products), "mainly modern" products (such as beverages, jute, chemicals and engineering), and a third class of industries labelled "mixed".

TABLE 2

DISTRIBUTION OF EMPLOYMENT BY INDUSTRY AND
TYPE OF ENTERPRISE, 1955

(thousands)

Industry	Household enterprises	Non-household below 10/20	10-49 with power, 20-99 without	50 or more with power, 100 or more without	All enterprises
Mainly traditional					
Foodstuffs	2,209	284	61	271	2,825
Tobacco products	240	160	66	97	563
Wool textiles	109	13	2	23	147
Silk textiles	149	76	31	32	288
Miscellaneous textiles	813	202	49	44	1,108
Wood and wood products	1,516	119	21	52	1,708
Leather and leather products	535	56	27	24	642
Miscellaneous	608	73	6	40	727
Total	6,179	983	263	583	8,008
Mixed					
Cotton textiles	2,725	316	41	843	3,925
Pottery, bricks, glass, etc.	813	160	59	204	1,236
Metals and products (excluding machinery)	732	83	28	328	1,171
Total	4,270	559	128	1,375	6,332
Mainly modern					
Beverages	177	27	14	439	657
Jute products	57	4	7	215	283
Paper and paper products	15	—	4	38	57
Printing and publishing	25	46	23	48	142
Chemicals	60	60	34	278	432
Machinery, electrical and transport equipment	106	41	22	112	291
Total	440	188	104	1,130	1,862
Grand Total	10,889	1,730	495	3,088	16,202

SOURCE: As for Table 1

The three industries in this middle group—cotton textiles, pottery, etc., and metals—are especially heterogeneous, containing within themselves both traditional products (such as handloom cloth, village pottery, brasswork, etc.) and the most modern products (such as mill-made textiles, sanitary wares and iron and steel).[3]

Although this classification of industries is rather rough and arbitrary, it does serve to illustrate the relation between type of product and type of enterprise. The great bulk of "mainly traditional" industries are carried on in household enterprises, while the majority of "mainly modern" products are produced by large-scale enterprises. It should also be noted that over half of the employment in the small factory group (10-49 with power, 20-99 without), is in traditional industries, and that only 11 per cent of employment in this group is in the two "ultra-modern" industries, engineering and chemicals.

The method of classifying enterprises which we have been using so far is convenient in some ways—for example, in distinguishing "household" from "non-household" small enterprises—but for most purposes, and especially for international comparisons, it is more satisfactory to classify enterprises by a single indicator of size. The simplest, and most commonly used, measure of size is the number of persons employed; and we have, therefore, made some estimates of the distribution of Indian manufacturing establishments (and of employment) by size of establishment on this basis. Table 3 shows the results of those calculations.

For firms employing 50 or more persons we have used the data published in *Occupational Pattern in Manufacturing Industries, 1956*.[4] For those below this level, we have made estimates, by interpolation on a double-logarithmic cumulative frequency distribution, adjusted in such a way as to produce roughly the right total number of establishments, which must itself be consistent with the estimated total number of persons employed. We have assumed that, in mid-1956, the total number of persons employed in manufacturing was about 16.5 million, of which 1.5 million would be absent from work on any given day. These—obviously very rough—assumptions yield a figure of 15 million persons employed in manufacturing on an average working day and a total

---

[3] There is, of course, an element of heterogeneity of product in all the industries listed; but it is more marked in these three cases.
[4] See note to Table 3 for reference.

TABLE 3

ESTIMATED SIZE DISTRIBUTION OF MANUFACTURING
ESTABLISHMENTS, 1956

Number of persons per establishment*	Number of establishments	Total number of persons employed (000)
Under 5	5,000,000	10,200
5 — 9	130,000	910
10 — 19	43,000	600
20 — 49	18,000	560
50 — 99	4,660	340
100 — 249	2,550	380
250 — 499	840	270
500 — 999	470	330
1,000 and over	580	1,410
Total	5,200,000	15,000

* Including working proprietors and unpaid family workers.

SOURCE: For establishments employing 50 or more: *Occupational Pattern in Manufacturing Industries, 1956,* Planning Commission, Government of India, 1959, pp. 45-46. For those below 50, see text.

number of manufacturing establishments of a little over 5 million. It should be noted, however, that a fairly wide variation of assumptions about the volume of total employment would have scarcely any effect on our estimates of the distribution of establishments employing 5 or more persons. This is important, because it is the shape of the distribution of establishments *above* the purely household level that matters. The number of "household" manufacturing establishments (and the total employment given by them) can, in any case, be measured only very arbitrarily.

If our estimated distribution of manufacturing establishments is compared with that given in *Occupational Pattern in Manufacturing Industries (OCMI)*, it will be found that our estimates for the two groups "10-19 employees" and "20-49 employees" are distinctly higher. For the 20-49 group our figure is 18,000 establishments compared with 10,000 in *OCMI* while for the 10-19 group our estimate is 43,000 establishments against less than 7,000 in *OCMI*. These discrepancies may be explained by the fact that the *OCMI* figures relate only to factories registered under the Factories Act. Thus, by comparison with our distribution, they exclude two types of small factory establishment: (1) all factories employing 10-19 *without* power; and (2) factories which *should* be registered but which were *not* registered. It is not possible to show conclusively that these two exclusions by the *OCMI* are sufficient to account for the discrepancies shown; but it is relevant to note that in 1948, the total number of factories employing 10-19 persons with power or 20 or more without power was estimated to amount to at least 40,000, although the actual number of factories of these types registered at that time was only 4,500.[5] And in 1956, the number registered in this group was still only 6,100, despite the introduction of the 1948 Act which *required* the states to register factories of these types. If, therefore, allowance is made for failures to register and also for the factories employing 10-19 *without* power (which are not obliged to register) there would seem to be no great difficulty in reconciling our estimates of the numbers of factories in the 10-49 group with those given by the *OCMI* or the factory inspectors.

For the purpose of further analysis, it will be convenient to define four main sizes of factory, as follows:

Description	*Definition* (Number employed)	*Average daily employment in 1956* (millions)
Household enterprises and small workshops	Less than 10 persons	11.1
Small factories	10-49 persons	1.2
Medium factories	50-499 persons	1.0
Large factories	500 or more persons	1.7

The official definition of a small enterprise was, until recently, one which employed less than 50 persons with power, or less than 100 without, *and* whose gross fixed capital had cost less than Rs. 5 lakhs. The definition has now been modified so as to exclude any reference to the number of employees, on the sensible grounds that,

[5] See *First Report of the National Income Committee,* Government of India, 1951, p. 73, footnote 80.

since one of the major objects of the small industries programme is to encourage employment, no restriction should be placed on the volume of employment given by a small enterprise. In practice, the programme has largely been directed, up to now, towards helping small *modern* firms which employ between 10 and 50 persons. These form part of the group defined by us as "small factories".

CHAPTER II

THE ARGUMENTS ADVANCED FOR ASSISTING SMALL ENTERPRISES

THE arguments most commonly advanced for encouraging the development of small enterprises in India fall into four main groups. First, there is the *employment* argument, which is based on the view that small enterprises are essentially "labour-intensive". Secondly, there is the *decentralisation* argument, which is based on the belief that small enterprises can more easily be dispersed into small towns or villages than large enterprises. Thirdly, there is a group of arguments which stress the *social* and *political* virtues of small enterprise, e. g. that small enterprises promote equality or democracy. And fourthly, there is the argument that small enterprises help to draw out *latent reserves* of scarce resources, especially of entrepreneurship and capital.

It happens that all these four arguments are mentioned in a single paragraph of the Industrial Policy Resolution of 1956. Referring to "the role of cottage and village and small-scale industries", the Resolution says :

"They provide immediate large scale employment ; they offer a method of ensuring a more equitable distribution of the national income and they facilitate an effective mobilisation of resources of capital and skill which might otherwise remain unutilised. Some of the problems that unplanned urbanisation tends to create will be avoided by the establishment of small centres of industrial production all over the country."[1]

To this should, perhaps, be added the well-known dictum of the Karve Committee, that "the principle of self-employment is at least as important to a successful democracy as that of self-government."[2]

We shall proceed to consider each of these four arguments in turn.

[1] Reprinted in *Second Five Year Plan,* Government of India, 1956, p. 47.
[2] *Report of the Village and Small-Scale Industries Committee,* Government of India, October 1955, p. 45.

THE "EMPLOYMENT" ARGUMENT

Although this argument is generally put forward in terms of the "employment" effects of establishing small enterprises, it cannot really be sustained in those terms. It is obvious that, if one wants to increase employment, there is no need to search for industries (or sizes of firms) that *require* a large amount of employment per unit of output. Employment as such can be "created" by simply adding on extra workers at any point one likes in the productive (or non-productive) process. The important problem, in other words, is not how to absorb *surplus* resources, but how to make the best use of *scarce* resources. If a solution can be found to the latter problem, output can be maximised ; and the distribution of the resulting income between the various members of the population—either by employment or by doles, or in other ways—is a secondary matter.[3]

If pressed, the advocates of the "employment" argument for promoting small enterprises will agree that their real meaning is that small enterprises maximise *output* from scarce capital and entrepreneurship, the giving of extra employment being, however, a necessary corollary. Hence, the "employment" argument is really an "output" argument. How does this "output" argument run?

The argument is that in countries where there is a large volume of unemployment and underemployment the cost of employing labour is much less to society than to private firms. From the private entrepreneur's point of view, wage payments are a cost of production, and only the profit remaining to him after making these payments is relevant to determining his investment decisions. But, from the social point of view, if the workers absorbed by an addition to productive capital would otherwise have been unemployed, the *whole* of the resulting addition to output (i. e. wages and profits) represents a surplus. The same conclusion follows also in the case of previously underemployed workers, if the loss of the net output, produced by them in their previous occupation, is automatically made

---

[3] In some cases, it is true, the method of allocating scarce resources other than labour may partly determine the distribution of labour income. But, in general, the first problem in an underdeveloped economy is to find out how to maximise output.

good by increased efforts on the part of the other previously underemployed workers who remain. Where a situation of this sort obtains—as it almost certainly does in India—the proper criterion for maximising the results of investment—from a social point of view—is not the marginal expected rate of *profit* on capital but the marginal expected rate of *net output* on capital.

There are, however, some qualifications that need to be made to this doctrine. The first is that, in counting the capital cost of creating new jobs, it is not sufficient to take account of the cost of the investment in factory buildings, machinery and working capital, but allowance must also be made for the cost of transporting, training and housing the new workers. When opportunities exist for choosing between different sizes or types of factory, or between different locations for an industry, such considerations as these may be extremely important. Another aspect that needs to be taken into account is the way in which the extra output is distributed. If, for example, investment is concentrated in small factories rather than in large factories, with the consequence that a larger proportion of the net output goes in wages, the overall rate of savings will be lower and the rate of growth of the economy will be slower. This is a social cost which must be offset against the social benefit arising from the chosen investment pattern.

But, the pure output argument for promoting small enterprises ignores these qualifications and bases itself on the proposition that the output-capital ratio for small enterprises is higher than for large enterprises. What evidence is there for the belief that this is so? Before we look at the evidence we must cross a *pons asinorum*. It is not, unfortunately, as rare a phenomenon as it should be for people to compare output-capital ratios for small firms in one group of industries (e. g. consumer goods) with those for large firms in another group of industries (e. g. capital goods). Such comparisons almost inevitably show a "favourable" result for small firms. But, of course, such comparisons prove nothing, except perhaps that consumer goods generally require less capital per unit of output than capital goods. Even this is often an irrelevant and misleading judgement, since the "capital" goods are usually essential to the production of the "consumer" goods.[4] It is clear that, if small enterprises are to be shown to use less capital per unit of output than larger enterprises, the comparison must be made between small and large enterprises *in the same industry* and, so far as possible, making practically the identical product.

Although the belief that small enterprises use less capital per unit of output than large enterprises is widespread, it is extremely difficult to find, either in India or elsewhere, relevant and reliable data which may serve to put the hypothesis to the test. We have, however, succeeded in bringing together a limited amount of relevant information. The first set of figures (given in Table 4) is derived from the *Census of Indian Manufactures, 1956.* The Census covers 29 "industries", some of which are fairly narrowly defined and homogeneous—such as sugar, cement or bicycles—while others are very wide agglomerations —such as glass and glassware, chemicals, or general engineering. For each industry, figures are published for various size groups of establishments, and it is from these that the ratios in Table 4 have been computed. Out of the 29 industries available only 10 have been selected for study : the others were rejected either because they seemed to be too heterogeneous in their products, or because they did not include a sufficient number of cases of both small and large factories to make a reasonable comparison possible.[5]

The underlying data, on which the figures in Table 4 are based, are far from ideal. The measurement of output (net value added) is, in principle, reasonably satisfactory ; the measurement of capital is not. Capital is measured in the Census by reference to the written down book value of fixed capital, as

---

[4] This is the case for a self-contained economy. In a trading economy there is usually some possibility of buying capital-intensive capital goods (and raw materials) from abroad and paying for them with capital-light consumer goods. But the scope for this sort of transaction is not as great as purely "theoretical" economists sometimes imagine. This is especially true of India in its present state of international trade.

[5] The Census covers only those factories which, on any day in the year, employed 20 or more "workers" with power. The term "worker", as defined in the Factories Act, includes all manual workers, and possibly a certain number of clerical and supervisory staff who are directly connected with the manufacturing process. Hence, the lower limit of the Census, in terms of total numbers employed, may be somewhat higher than 20.

entered in the firm's accounts, plus the value of stocks, plus cash in hand and at the banks. Fortunately, the figure for cash is not large, amounting for all industries combined to only about 5 per cent of the total capital. But the book values of fixed capital are based on historical costs, and the methods of depreciation may vary from firm to firm.

TABLE 4

OUTPUT-CAPITAL RATIOS IN DIFFERENT SIZES OF FACTORY, 1956

Industry	Average daily number of employees				
	20-49	50-99	100-249	250-499	500 and over
Wheat flour	0.23	0.44	0.35	0.80	—
Rice milling	0.32	0.34	0.30	(0.24)	—
Vegetable oils	0.20	0.24	0.22	0.30	(0.31)
Soap	0.13	0.18	0.55	(0.09)	0.71
Tanning	0.28	0.39	0.38	0.55	(0.32)
Cotton textiles (spinning and weaving)	0.24	0.50	0.23	0.41	0.63
Woollen textiles	0.14	0.34	0.16	0.34	0.51
Bicycles	0.51	0.58	0.39	0.51	0.49
Electric fans	0.36	0.33	0.53	0.41	0.30

SOURCE: *Census of Indian Manufactures, 1956.*
    Figures in brackets relate to one factory only.
    Output=annual net value added. Capital=net fixed capital at book value plus stocks and cash, at end of year.

Nevertheless, for want of better information, we believe that the figures in Table 4 are worthy of study. They present a rather remarkable picture. Out of the 10 industries in the table it will be seen that in five cases the output-capital ratio tends to *increase* with the size of factory, while in the remaining five it stays fairly constant, or oscillates about its average level. In *no single case* is there a clear tendency for the output-capital ratio to *fall* with the size of factory.

In interpreting these figures two objections may be raised. First, it may be objected that the Census data start from too high a level: they exclude the really small factories, in which the output-capital ratio is larger. There is, probably, some truth in this objection, as we shall see; but, it cannot upset the conclusion that, for factories employing about 20 or more persons, there is no distinct trend favouring the smaller size groups. The second objection turns on the method of valuing capital. We have already referred to the unsatisfactory nature of the data. At the same time, there is no particular reason for believing that the method of measuring capital from the accounts should produce an upward bias in the valuation of capital for small factories or a downward bias in its valuation for large factories.

A second source of information is available in studies (prepared by the Perspective Planning Division of the Planning Commission) of capital, labour and output relations in various industries. Some of these studies refer to "organised industries" (establishments employing 50 or more with power or 100 or more without power), while others relate to "small factories" (below this level). Out of 149 organised industries covered in one study and 172 small factories covered in another it has been possible to match 15 cases where the two industries appear to be making the "same" product.[6] Output-capital ratios for these 15 industries are given in Table 5.

Unlike the Census figures, which record actual results for a particular year, the figures in Table 5 are based on *ex ante* estimates of what can be produced with given amounts of initial capital. The estimates for the small factories were originally derived from certain "Model Schemes", prepared by the Small Scale Industries Organisation; those for the large factories are taken from various sources, but primarily from information collected by the Development Wing of the Ministry of Commerce and Industry regarding plans for expansion by large-scale units in the private sector. It will be seen that for the large factories two sets of estimates are given, the first being based on the assumption that the factory will operate the same number of shifts as is normal in that industry (in most cases, only one) and the second being based on a "desirable" number of shifts (generally two). For large factories it is reasonable to

[6] The large factory data come from "A Study of Economic Coefficients for Organised Industries in India", and the small factory data from "The Capital and Labour Requirements of Small Factories", both produced (in mimeograph) by the Perspective Planning Division of the Planning Commission.

consider what can be achieved by varying the number of shifts, while in the case of small factories, which are usually run by one or two proprietors, there are generally great difficulties in the way of working more than one shift.

TABLE 5

COMPARATIVE OUTPUT-CAPITAL RATIOS IN SMALL AND LARGE FACTORIES

Product	Small factory (Not more than 50 employed) One shift basis	Large factory (50 or more employed)	
		Present shift basis†	"Desirable" shift basis‡
Fruit and vegetable preservation	0.25	0.30	0.42
Leather footwear	0.33	0.52	0.68
Cycle tyres and tubes	0.46	0.61*	0.61
Superphosphate	0.28	0.45*	0.45*
Matches	0.29	0.87	1.10
Sanitary wares and related products	0.53	0.35	0.54
Steel furniture	0.54	0.48	0.66
Tin containers	0.47	0.48	0.66
Bolts and nuts	0.50	0.48	0.66
Sewing machines	0.57	0.97*	0.97*
PVC insulated cables	0.26	0.55	0.67
Storage batteries	0.54	0.57	0.73
Radio sets	0.52	0.56	0.72
Refrigerators	0.68	0.32	0.47
Bicycles	0.46	0.57	0.71

SOURCE: See text.

Output=annual gross value added. Capital=initial outlay on fixed and working capital, including required cash balance.

† In all cases except those marked with an asterisk this means one shift. An asterisk means three shifts.

‡ In all cases except those marked with an asterisk this means two shifts. An asterisk means three shifts.

The figures in Table 5 tell much the same story as those in Table 4. Out of 15 cases there are five in which the large factory clearly has a higher output-capital ratio, even on a one-shift basis. In addition the three large factories whose present basis of operation is three shifts all show higher output-capital ratios than the corresponding small factories. Against this, there are only three cases in which the large factory has a less favourable output-capital ratio on a one-shift basis; and in two of these the large factory's disadvantage disappears if it is operated on a two-shift basis. In the middle, there are four cases where the one-shift ratios are approximately the same for both large and small factories but where the two-shift large factory ratio is clearly more advantageous. The conclusions, which emerge from these figures, are striking enough as they stand ; but, they could be made even more convincing if account were taken of the fact that *in practice* small factories generally work at a lower level of capacity than large factories. Thus the *ex post* ratios for large and small factories of the types listed might well turn out to be even less favourable to small factories than those actually shown, which are based on the assumption of full capacity operation.

None of the "small factories" represented in Table 5 employs more than 50 persons ; they are mostly in the 20-49 range. So it may be argued that we have still not thrown any light on the output-capital ratios of factories employing less than 20 persons. For this purpose we are obliged to turn to such survey data as is available.

We have used two main sources : the National Sample Survey and the Delhi survey of small-scale industries. The relevant NSS report is Number 19, *Report on Small Scale Manufacture*, which refers to the period October 1953 to March 1954. This report covers households which carried on a manufacturing or handicraft business, either on a proprietory or partnership basis, and which were below the Factories Act limits. The all-India sample included 10,000 households of these types. Unfortunately, the authors of the report appeared to feel that a sample of this size could not safely be broken down to give results for particular industries. So only their aggregate estimates for all manufacturing industries are available for analysis.

The report contains figures of average gross monthly value added per household establishment and of gross fixed capital at original cost. One in five of the households, which had inherited their buildings, could give no estimate of the original cost of those buildings. We have made allowance for the value of these buildings (on the assumption that they had the same average original cost as the buildings used by the other households), and also for working capital at 12 per cent of gross sales value (this ratio being based on an estimate derived from the Delhi survey). In these assumptions, the overall annual output-capital ratio works out at 0.84.[7] For comparison with the figures in Table 5, however, it is desirable to make some allowance for the increase in the price level of fixed capital since the time of installation. It does not seem to be an unreasonable assumption that the average age of the buildings and equipment covered by the survey was at least 15 years ; and, in the light of the rise in the general price level in that period, we shall not be over-estimating the replacement cost in 1953-54 if we add on 50 per cent of the value of fixed capital. This would bring the output-capital ratio down to 0.63. If we were to double the value of fixed capital, the ratio would fall to 0.5. The "true" output-capital ratio, when capital is measured at replacement cost, probably lies between these limits.

Before we consider the implication of these results, let us turn to the Delhi survey. This survey covered 326 small manufacturing units, employing between 2 to 19 persons, with a minimum gross fixed capital of Rs. 250. The sample was drawn from official lists of small businesses, out of which thirteen reasonably homogeneous industries were selected for study. The data collected relate to the year 1953-54.[8]

From this survey, also, estimates can be made of value added and of fixed and working capital employed, on a roughly comparable basis with those presented in Table 5. For some enterprises it was necessary to make an allowance for the capital value of rented premises, which we took arbitrarily at ten times their annual gross rental. The ratio which can most conveniently be calculated from the data is that of *net* value added to total capital, the fixed capital component being valued at current replacement cost. The ratios for the thirteen industries are found to range from 0.31 for flour mills to 1.37 for trunks. A crude average, implicitly weighted by the capital engaged in each industry, comes to 0.57. On a *gross* value added basis the average output-capital ratio would be about 0.6.

[7] For these calculations monthly average gross value added per establishment has been multiplied by 12, despite the slight danger of seasonal effects. The figures used exclude four industries : Pan, bidi, laundry services and hotel keeping. The data appear on pp. 34 and 36 of the report.

[8] For further details see P. N. Dhar, *Small-Scale Industries in Delhi,* Asia Publishing House, 1958.

Taking the NSS results and the Delhi survey's figures together, it seems that the *average* gross output-capital ratio for firms employing less than 20 persons may be somewhere in the region of 0.6. This is significantly higher than the average *ex ante* ratio for the Model Schemes, which is about 0.5 on the assumption of full capacity operation and about 0.4 on the assumption of 75 per cent capacity operation.[9] It is unfortunate that we cannot make a closer comparison of particular industries; at best, we can relate a few of the industries listed in Table 5 to the roughly corresponding industries covered in the Delhi survey. These comparisons tend to confirm the general impression that very small firms have a more favourable output-capital ratio than those recommended in the Model Schemes. But, when they are compared with large factories operating on two or three shifts the outcome is indeterminate.

The conclusions which seem to emerge from these comparisons are : (1) for factories which employ 20 or more persons the output-capital ratios *increase* with size of unit, while (2) for enterprises employing less than 20 persons the output-capital ratio is generally more favourable than for those immediately above them, but not necessarily more favourable than for large enterprises working two or three shifts. The figures suggest that, in general, the *most capital-intensive* type of manufacturing establishment is the small factory using modern machinery, and employing up to 50 workers. This is a somewhat disturbing conclusion when we remember that it is precisely factories of this sort which are now being promoted by the Small Scale Industries Organisation, especially in the industrial estates.

These conclusions will, no doubt, seem very perverse to those who have taken it for granted that "small industries" always use less capital and more labour than large enterprises. Yet they are not really so surprising, once the essential distinction between *traditional* and *modern* types of industry is clearly grasped. Traditional industries are those that use traditional techniques and, since traditional techniques are generally capital-saving and labour-using, traditional industries tend to have favourable output-capital ratios. But once we move into modern industry, we are in a different technical world. In this world although large factories sometimes employ more elaborate techni-

9 "The Capital and Labour Requirements of Small Factories", p. 8.

ques than small factories, *all* are modern and mechanised. There is no such technical gulf between the small electric motor factory and the large electric motor factory as there is between *gur* and sugar making, or between bullock carts and bicycles. Moreover, *within* modern industry increase in the size of the enterprise is accompanied not only by technical changes but also by economies of scale. It frequently happens, in other words, that large factories can produce the same volume of output by using less labour *and* less capital than would be used by small factories.

THE DECENTRALISATION ARGUMENT

This argument generally runs along the following lines: (1) Decentralisation is desirable because large cities become congested, filled with slums and costly to run. If people could be kept in the villages and smaller towns, there would be less need for new housing and other social construction, and the people would enjoy a better life. Apart from this, various social and political arguments are advanced for trying to avoid a "malconcentration" of population in big cities.

(2) If these aims are to be achieved, it is not enough to put a wall round the big cities: counter-attractions must be created in the smaller places. One important counter-attraction would be to establish industries there, which would give the local people decent jobs without their having to move to the cities. This would also avoid the unfortunate related effects of migration, in particular the drawing away of the most active and enterprising people (especially young people) from the countryside.

(3) "Small industries" can more easily be decentralised than "large industries". There should, therefore, be a drive to spread out "small industries" into small towns and villages.

It is not within the scopes of this paper to enter into any detailed consideration of steps (1) and (2) in the above argument. On the whole, we agree that large cities should not be allowed to become very much larger. If this is to be done, however, it will be necessary to take positive measures to slow down the trend, both by putting obstacles in the way of the establishment of more industry in large cities, and by encouraging the establishment of new industry in other places. But it does not follow that the *only* alternative to the further growth of the large cities is the industrialisation of small towns (less than, say, 10,000 population) and villages. This seems to be an unnecessary jump from one extreme to the other. At the 1951 Census there were 71 cities with a population of 100,000 or more, 111 towns with a population of 50-100,000, and 401 towns with a population of 20-50,000. At present there must be well over 600 towns and cities of 20,000 or more. Since it is in towns of this size that some infra-structure may be available, it is mainly amongst them that the most suitable places can be found for the development of new industrial centres.

But let us pass from this question to the more immediately relevant issue, which is posed in step (3) above. It is clear that the crux of the argument, as it affects "small industry", lies in this last step. Is there any evidence for the belief that "small industries can more easily be decentralised than large industries"? Here again, as in previous discussions, we must focus attention on the distinction between traditional and modern enterprises. The traditional enterprises, by their very nature, are already largely "decentralised" : they started in the villages and most of them— as we saw in Table 1—are still there. Thus, so long as one automatically thinks of these industries, whenever someone mentions the phrase "small industries", it will seem obvious that "small industries" are easily "decentralised". "Small industries" are indeed often referred to in official documents as "the decentralised sector", and presumably this is what the authors have in mind.

But what of the *modern* small enterprises? Do they also belong to the "decentralised sector"? We saw in Table 1 that small enterprises employing between 10 and 49 workers with power, or between 20 and 99 workers without power, contain a higher proportion of urban workers than any of the other three groups of firms. A breakdown of this group, by industry, also shows that of the employees of enterprises of this size who are in the two leading modern industries, chemicals and engineering (including metals), less than a quarter live in rural areas. If metals were also excluded the proportion would fall to one-seventh. It seems, therefore, that small modern enterprises—far from being "decentralised"—are almost entirely located in towns, and for the most part in the large cities. There are important reasons for this. As pointed out earlier, small modern firms generally draw their raw materials from long distances and sell their products in fairly wide markets. In the case of consumer goods, the types of goods made by these modern firms are usually in the "luxury" class, in the sense that they are not items of everyday consumption on which any large proportion of the average household budget is spent. Almost inevitably, therefore, enterprises making such goods must sell in a wide market, containing populations which run into millions rather than into thousands. Such firms cannot be expected to survive in remote villages by working for the "local market". As for enterprises which make producer goods, the case for their being close to large urban markets, in which their main customers are located, is too obvious to be worth stating.

Our conclusion on this argument is, therefore, that so far as traditional village industries are concerned it is true, but not very helpful. If village industries could flourish, villages would, of course, be better places to live in. The real difficulty is to know how to revive and strengthen village industries. As we have seen above, a fair case can be made for the promotion of village industries on the grounds of their favourable output-capital ratio. And this case becomes even stronger if the proposal is merely to make full use of the *existing* capacity of village industries (e. g. handlooms). But if village industries are to grow, the demand for their products must somehow be stimulated. To some extent a general improvement in agriculture—which is essential for other reasons —will raise the rural demand for the services of village artisans. At the same time, unfortunately, a rise in per capita rural incomes will tend to divert rural demand away from the products of village industries (many of which are "inferior" in the economic sense), towards the products of modern industry. This trend can only be arrested or reversed by imposing special taxes or restrictions on the competing modern products, or by giving subsidies to village industries (as is now being done to stimulate the demand for khadi, handloom cloth, handmade matches, etc.). But the imposition of discriminatory taxes—or the giving of subsidies— *changes* the output-capital ratio in a direction unfavourable to the assisted industries, and, at the margin, changes it very substantially. Before accepting a programme of this sort, therefore, it is necessary to review carefully the net return in terms of value added for the additional capital outlays involved.[10]

[10] For example, even in the case of the handloom industry, where the case for assistance is at its strongest, it appears that out of total current

Even if, after carrying out this exercise, it can be shown that the marginal output-capital ratio for traditional village industries is higher than for modern industries, objection can still be made to the programme on the grounds that the savings (and taxes) that will be generated by a large number of very small incomes will be substantially less than those that would be generated by an equal (or even smaller) income in the hands of fewer people. This point will be discussed further under the next "argument".

An alternative approach to the problem of rural industrialisation is the suggestion that village industries should gradually be *modernised*. Wherever electricity is available it is, of course, perfectly feasible to encourage village artisans to install a few power tools, to convert handlooms into powerlooms, and so on. This is, indeed, a process which is bound to develop as time goes on. Whether this process should be *encouraged* is, however, a difficult issue, since the mechanisation of village industries will undoubtedly produce "technological unemployment" in the first instance. A further problem is whether mechanised units for processing local raw materials should be developed in villages or in small local urban centres. In most cases one mechanised unit—even on a small scale—would be sufficient to serve the needs of several villages, and it would most logically be located at a central point within that group of villages. Inevitably, the same centre would, in course of time, tend to attract to itself most of the local industry, so that the villages would gradually lose even the small industries that they now have. In the meantime, of course, the original undifferentiated rural area would have acquired a small industrial centre of its own. But the goal of industrialising the village as such would have been missed. Perhaps, after all, that goal is really a mirage.

As regards the decentralisation of modern industry it appears

net earnings by handloom weavers of about Rs. 60 crores over half is contributed by the Government, if we include both the direct subsidies paid and the indirect subsidies given by placing differential taxes on mill cloth. If, as is possible, half the present sales of handloom cloth could be maintained, even if all subsidies were withdrawn and the market price was adjusted so as to give the weavers the same average return per yard as at present, then the marginal effect of the programme of assistance to the handloom industry—in terms of the net addition to output—is negligible, and it becomes merely an elaborate method of distributing money to the unemployed.

that the first task is to develop several hundred of India's large and medium-sized towns as flourishing regional centres of industry. In order to achieve this objective, it will not be sufficient to concentrate on developing "small industries" by, for example, putting up industrial estates.   Small firms are, in fact, more dependent on the external economies of a good local market, good supplies of raw materials from local dealers, and so on, than large and medium firms.   Hence, if pioneering work is to be done, it should be the larger firms—whether from the public or the private sector —that should lead the way.   If the Government is serious about decentralisation then it must be prepared to persuade large firms to go to some of these underdeveloped towns.   Small firms will soon follow, to some extent automatically, and even quicker if they are given encouragement by the provision of suitable facilities. But the first step should be to move some major industries into these places.[11]

THE SOCIAL AND POLITICAL ARGUMENTS

These arguments fall broadly into two sub-groups. First, there are the arguments that hinge round the idea of *equality*. It is suggested, for example, that in small enterprises there is less of a gap, economically and socially, between the worker and his employer than in large enterprises. Sometimes it is said that there is less "exploitation" in small firms. A further argument, in this sub-group, is that the development of a large number of small enterprises, in place of a few large enterprises, will reduce the spread between the highest and the lowest incomes and avoid an undesirable concentration of economic power.

The second sub-group is concerned with the problem of *democracy*. It is suggested that the existence of a large number of independent self-employed persons is a guarantee of the maintenance of democratic institutions, an obstacle to the domination of trade unions, and a barrier to communism.

[11] Of course, many large enterprises have been and are being set up in remote rural areas where their raw materials happen to be located (e. g. the steel plants). These places should rapidly develop into new towns, to which both medium and smaller enterprises will be attracted by the local market and supply of skilled manpower and materials, leading to the development of a number of new industrial centres.

We shall not attempt to analyse this second sub-group of arguments in detail, since they are outside the economic field, with which we are primarily concerned. In any case, it is doubtful whether the evidence that can be adduced to support, or to reject, these arguments is amenable to fully objective examination. If we may express a personal view, it is that there is, on the whole, less political stability in countries in which "self-employment" is most prevalent than in those countries in which the bulk of industry is organised in large-scale enterprises. If, moreover, in order to increase the number of self-employed it proves necessary to give them Government subsidies, protection and so forth, this will hardly be likely to create a class of sturdy independent-minded citizens.

On the "equality" argument there is more to be said. First, it is undoubtedly true that the incomes arising in a large number of small firms will be both more numerous and, on the average, smaller than those which would be paid out by a few large firms producing the same output. In general, wages in small firms are lower than in large firms; profit per unit of capital is also lower; and, since the volume of capital owned by each employer is smaller, small firms will not produce any "millionaire" incomes. But there are two disadvantages to be set against these arguments, both of which relate to the "dynamic" aspects of the economy. The first is that the total volume of savings and taxes which is generated by a large number of small incomes is almost inevitably smaller than the volume generated by an equal total income in the hands of a smaller number of people; and the second is that small firms are, generally, not so technically progressive as large firms. For both these reasons, therefore, the choice of greater *present equality* may hinder the rapid *growth* of the economy, and hence postpone the attainment of a higher standard of living for the whole population in the future. This is one of a number of cases in which present benefits have to be weighed against future benefits. On this type of issue only the collective will of the population, as expressed through their political leaders, can decide.[12]

[12] In principle, in a perfectly competitive economy the choice between the present and the future would be settled in the capital market and would be reflected in the level of the rate of interest. Such a situation is, however, unlikely to exist in India. Even the perfectly competitive

Our second comment is concerned with the question of "exploitation". We do not know exactly what this argument means; but if it means that workers in small firms are better off than workers in large firms, it is certainly not true. It is interesting in this connection to consider the figures in Table 6.

TABLE 6

AVERAGE WAGE AND SALARY PAYMENTS PER EMPLOYEE IN DIFFERENT SIZES OF FACTORIES IN FOUR COUNTRIES

(Index numbers: Factories employing 1,000 and over = 100)

Number of employees per factory	India 1955	Japan 1952	Britain 1949	U.S.A. 1947
4 - 9 (5 - 9)	...	39	...	73*
10-19 (11-24)	47	46	84*	79*
20-49 (25-49)	51	53	83*	84
50-99	55	60	84	86
100-199 (100-249)	72*	69	85	86*
200-499 (250-499)	85*	83	86	88*
500-999	88	96	89	90
1,000 & over	100	100	100	100

*Figure relates to size group shown in brackets.
SOURCES India : *Census of Indian Manufactures, 1955.*
Other countries : "Statistical Analysis of Medium and Small Enterprises in Japan", *Asian Affairs,* 1957, p. 217.

They suggest that there is a common tendency, in all countries, for the average wage (or salary) payment to be lower in small factories than in large factories. There are various possible reasons for this. It does not necessarily follow that the average payment *for the same kind of work* is everywhere lower in small firms than in large firms. What is noticeable, however, is that in advanced industrialised countries, such as Britain or the United States, the wage and salary "differential" between large and small factories is much smaller than in less developed countries, such as India and Japan. The probable explanation for this is that in less developed countries the great pressure of unemployment, combined with the existence of fairly strong

market can, of course, only balance demands and supplies within a given framework of property and income distribution.

trade unions in larger firms, leads to an intensive struggle for jobs in the smaller enterprises. Small enterprises in India and Japan pay, on the average, only half as much per person as large factories employing 1,000 persons or more. According to one's taste, one may deplore the fact that small factories pay so little, or praise them for adjusting themselves so intelligently to the pressures of the free market. But one can scarcely find support here for the view that small enterprises reduce the degree of "exploitation".

Our conclusion about this group of arguments is that, apart from certain political aspects (which are outside our province), the only important argument in favour of small enterprises is that they spread the total income generated more widely over the population. As against this, we have noted that the price of greater equality now may be a smaller income in the future or, to put it another way, the price of more (lower paid) jobs now may be fewer "decent jobs" later.

THE LATENT RESOURCES ARGUMENT

Although this argument is the least often mentioned, it is probably the most important. In India there are acute shortages of skilled entrepreneurs, managers and workers, and also of capital. If there are anywhere latent reserves of these scarce factors, which can reasonably easily be brought to light or rapidly developed, then the matter deserves immediate attention.

The argument in relation to small enterprises is threefold :

(1) There are large numbers of small employers who have the capacity—given suitable opportunity and perhaps with a little assistance—to manage larger or more efficient enterprises.

(2) There are even larger numbers of *potential* entrepreneurs, whose abilities are not at present being made use of.

(3) There are reserves of idle savings which could be drawn into productive use if the owners had the chance to set up business on their own account.

Of these three arguments the last seems to be of comparatively little importance. The only hoards whose "mobilisation" would be of any overall advantage to the community would be hoards of precious metals or other exportable commodities. If there are indeed potential businessmen—or their financiers—who would be willing to sell gold in order to invest in a small business, this would be a definite gain to the economy.[13] What we are doubtful about is whether the amount of dishoarding that could be induced in this way would be significant. There is really no evidence either way ; but it seems unlikely that more than a very small fraction of the funds put into new small businesses come from sales of gold. In any case, any such funds represent only a once-for-all gain. In the long run it is the effect on the propensity to save that is more important. On this point we have already expressed the view that larger firms generate more savings (and tax revenues), out of a given total income, than small firms.

The real strength of the "latent resources" argument seems to us to lie in the proposition that there are latent reserves of entrepreneurial skill. The point can be made, as we have said, either in relation to new (or *potential*) entrepreneurs or in relation to "underemployed" entrepreneurs. We propose now to examine this problem.

The first question to which we may address ourselves is the following : Is there reason to believe that India suffers from an *overall shortage* of entrepreneurs? We may first seek to answer this question by considering the rewards paid to entrepreneurs, or the degree to which India depends on foreign entrepreneurship. On both these criteria, it seems to us that, while there is evidence of a shortage of *efficient* entrepreneurs, especially those capable of running medium or large enterprises, there is no *overall* shortage. Taking India as a whole, there is a very large supply of *small* entrepreneurs who are willing to try their hand at manufacturing industry. It is true that this supply comes mainly from a few areas—Bombay, West Bengal and Punjab in particular—and this may be the cause of some difficulties in other areas, unless there is free mobility of entrepreneurs throughout the country ; but provided this problem can be overcome, the supply of small entrepreneurs for the country as a whole is not inadequate.

---

[13] If imports of gold could be completely eliminated there would not be much gain ; but as things stand, an increase in the internal supply of gold—by dishoarding—would tend to reduce smuggling.

TABLE 7

ESTIMATED SIZE DISTRIBUTIONS OF MANUFACTURING
ESTABLISHMENTS AND OF EMPLOYMENT IN
MANUFACTURING IN FOUR COUNTRIES

(Establishments employing 10 and over only)

Number of employees per establishment	Percentage of establishments				Percentage of employment			
	India 1956	Japan 1953	Britain 1956	U.S.A. 1955	India 1956	Japan 1953	Britain 1956	U.S.A. 1955
10 - 19	61.4	55.3	36.8	32.2	15.4	16.1	6.3	3.9
20 - 49	25.7	29.6	32.6	32.2	14.4	19.2	10.8	8.8
50 - 99	6.7	8.4	14.7	16.2	8.7	11.8	11.5	10.5
100 - 249	3.6	4.2	9.5	11.4	9.8	13.0	16.1	15.6
250 - 499	1.2	1.3	3.4	4.5	6.9	8.8	12.5	14.0
500 - 999	0.7	0.7	1.8	2.0	8.5	10.3	13.0	12.5
1,000 and over	0.8	0.5	1.2	1.5	36.3	20.8	29.8	34.7
Total	100.0	100.0	100.0	100.0	100.0	100.0	100.0	100.0
Equivalent numbers (000)	70	85	95	140	3,890	4,090	8,870	15,850
Approximate number for establishments employing less than 10 persons (000)	5,000	320	120	150	12,000	1,100	400	500

SOURCES : India : *Occupational Pattern in Manufacturing Industries, India, 1956,* Government of India, Planning Commission, 1959.
National Sample Survey, Report Number 16, *Employment and Unemployment,* Ninth Round, May-November 1955.

Japan : *The Smaller Industry in Japan,* Asia Kyokai, 1957.
"Statistical Analysis of Medium and Small Enterprises in Japan", *Asian Affairs,* 1957.

Great Britain: *Annual Abstract of Statistics,* No. 93, London.

U.S.A. : *Statistical Abstract of the United States, 1957,* Washington, D.C.

In this connection it is of interest to compare the size distributions of manufacturing establishments given in Table 7, in which data from four countries—India, Japan, Britain and the United States—are brought together. In order to exclude the effect of the enormously large number of household establishments in India, we have confined the comparison to establishments employing 10 or more persons.[14]   There are several points of interest to be noted.   First, India is seen to have quite a large total number of establishments above the 10-person limit. It is true that, in relation to population, the stock of establishments in India is not as large as in the other countries ; but in relation to the existing volume of manufacturing output it is more than adequate[15]   One of the reasons for this is that Indian establishments are very much concentrated in the smallest size group (10-19 persons employed).   On an average, Indian establishments, employing 10 or more persons, employ only 55 persons.   This is a little more than the Japanese average (48 persons), but it is much below the British or American figures (93 and 113 respectively).

A peculiarity of the Indian distribution is that, while it has a high concentration of *establishments* in the lowest size group, it has a high concentration of *employees* in the highest size group.   Indian industry tends to be either on a very small scale or on a very large scale ; and it is somewhat thin in the middle.[16] The phenomenon can doubtless be explained in terms of the "colonial" nature of the Indian economy : large foreign firms, and their Indian imitators, come in at the top, while small indigenous entrepreneurs crowd in at the bottom[17]   But, whatever

[14] To make the data comparable it has been necessary to undertake some graphic interpolations.   The coverage of the figures may not be strictly identical in each country, especially in respect of the inclusion or exclusion of enterprises which are both "manufacturers" and providers of services, e. g. garages ; but for establishments employing 10 or more persons this is not likely to be an important matter.

[15] To take an extreme case, India, with half as many establishments of 10 and over as the United States, produces in those establishments only about one-fortieth of the value of the net output produced by equivalent-sized American establishments.

[16] If establishments were to be classified on the basis of net output—instead of by employment size—it would no longer be true that the proportion of output (or employment) in the highest size group is greater in India than in the United States or Great Britain ; but the Indian distribution would still be "thin in the middle".

[17] An analysis of schemes for the establishment and expansion of manufacturing enterprises approved during the first few years of the Second Plan suggests that this process of "polarisation" may be intensifying.

may be the origin of the peculiarity, it suggests that there may be scope for encouraging the development of more *medium-sized* firms in India. This is rather an important conclusion, for, the *medium-sized* firm (say, 50-499 employees), is very often close to the optimum size, especially in the lighter manufacturing trades. It is small enough to be manageable without the employment of a large overhead staff ; but it is also large enough to take advantage of the essential economies of large-scale operation. Too little attention has so far been given to this type of firm, which has an important role to play in the future of Indian development.[18] It is worth noting, in this connection, that in Japan a "small" enterprise is usually defined as one which employs less than 200 persons ; and increasingly the Japanese are beginning to think in terms of the "small-medium" enterprise.

To return to the question of "latent resources", it is our view that there is no evidence of an overall shortage of *small* entrepreneurs in India, and in that sense there is no great need to search for latent resources of small entrepreneurship. Nevertheless, there is a good case for trying to make the path of new entrepreneurship as smooth as possible (though we would not favour some current proposals which seem to be designed to turn it into a "primrose path"). In addition, there is a need to attract entre-

Out of 90 *new units* approved by the Development Wing (all in the size class 50 and above), 31 were expected to employ 500 or more, compared with an existing distribution in which, out of 90 factories employing 50 or more, only 10 would employ 500 or more. Meanwhile, of course, some small firms must have been expanding gradually into the medium range ; but, amongst the "substantial expansions" of firms employing 50 or more (which also required a licence), more than half were expected to involve an *addition* to employment of 500 or more. (Data obtained from "Investment-Output-Employment Relationships, Phasing of Investments and Time Lags in Organised Manufacturing Industry", Perspective Planning Division, Planning Commission, March 1960. As a result of considerable non-response to the inquiry the data may be biased ; but they are unlikely to be so biased as to invalidate the conclusion suggested above.)

[18] Implicitly the Government has recognised the need to permit the growth of medium-sized firms by steadily relaxing the definition of a small enterprise. Under the present definition—which places an upper limit of Rs. 5 lakhs on gross fixed capital—firms employing 100 or even more persons (on double-shift) can come within the ambit of the small industries programme.

preneurs to certain areas where the supply is at present inadequate. Obstacles to the internal migration of entrepreneurs
should, so far as possible, be eliminated ; and there may be a
case for offering positive inducements to migration to some
areas. Apart from this, however, the main lesson of our study
of this problem is that there is a need for more firms of medium
size, because the capital-intensive techniques which characterise
modern small enterprises can, in many cases, be fully productive only if they are worked on a larger scale than at present.
Any positive measures that can be taken to promote the *growth*
of small firms into efficient medium-sized firms will, therefore,
be of great advantage to the economy.

AN ALTERNATIVE APPROACH TO SMALL
ENTERPRISE POLICY

It may seem that the implication of the above discussion is
that, with the possible exception of some village industry programmes, there is little or no justification for special efforts to
assist the development of small enterprises. We do not propose
to enter here into a more detailed discussion of the wisdom or
otherwise of attempting to bolster up village industries. We
have drawn attention above to some of the difficult questions that need to be resolved before such programmes can
be justified on purely economic grounds. In this paper we
are primarily concerned with programmes for assisting small
modern enterprises.

So far as modern industry is concerned it is our view that,
on the basis of the available evidence, there is no good case for
giving small enterprises *preferential* treatment. But, even if we
abandon the notion that small enterprises have a *special virtue
in themselves*, this does not exclude the possibility that there
may be good reasons for establishing a programme of assistance
to small enterprises. Small enterprises form a large part of the
industrial population of India. They suffer from many deficiencies : most of them are technically backward and financially
weak, their products are often sub-standard, they are inefficient
in their use of labour, and they provide inadequate incomes
both for their employees and for their owners. On the other
hand, many of these small entrepreneurs have latent potentiali-

ties of improvement. If they are helped to overcome their difficulties, they may succeed in raising their standards, increasing their outputs and eventually make a fuller contribution to India's industrial development. It is this approach to the matter which, we believe, should form the true basis of small enterprise policy. The difference between this approach and the accepted one is rather like the difference between a policy of encouraging the production of children (on the grounds that children are desirable in themselves), and a policy which, while leaving the production of children to follow its natural course, concentrates on the *better education* of the child population. Just as the child is father of the man, so the small firm is the source from which many medium and larger firms can grow. And even without changing its size the small firm can become a more useful member of society.

In practice, this difference of approach is largely a matter of emphasis. Most of the programmes already established would continue (some of them, indeed, would be strengthened). But others would be pruned or redirected to a greater or lesser degree. Above all, some of the proposals which are now being pressed with increasing vigour, such as the location of a large proportion of new industrial estates in rural areas, or the establishment of reserved quotas for small firms in a number of industries, would be resisted. The basic difference between the two approaches may, perhaps, be expressed in the following terms. The existing approach tends more and more to give special *favours* (preferences, subsidies, reserved areas etc.) to small firms ; the alternative approach would aim, rather, to *remove their disabilities*. It is true that it is not always easy to draw a clear line between removing a disability and conferring a positive advantage. But, the difference of approach is nevertheless important. For example, since small firms are often technically backward, we would try to remove this disability by offering them technical advice and help ; but beyond a certain point such advice should be charged for. Again, since small firms lack capital, we would try to provide the necessary institutional channels to give them access to capital, but not at a subsidised price ; if they lack marketing contacts, we would help them to establish such contacts, but without taking over responsibility for selling their products ; if they lack good premises, we would put up industrial estates, but not at heavily subsidised rents.

In the next two sections of this paper we shall survey some of the major current programmes for helping small enterprises ; and we shall consider to what degree current policies might be modified to bring them into line with the alternative "disability-removing" approach that has been suggested above. The first of these sections will be devoted to a study of the industrial estates programme, which is an increasingly important constituent of the whole programme ; and in the second section we shall consider more briefly the other main instruments of policy. In none of this will there be any reference, except in passing, to the large programmes now in existence for assisting traditional industries (handloom, village industries, etc.), since a study of these programmes would require a major work in itself. We shall confine our attention to the policies for helping small *modern* firms, which come under the official direction of the Small Scale Industries Board.

CHAPTER III

THE INDUSTRIAL ESTATES
PROGRAMME

INTRODUCTION

ONE of the principal inhibiting factors with which the small
industrialist has to contend is lack of suitable factory space with
adequate facilities for water and power. Acquiring land, buildings and other facilities not only takes a great deal of time and
energy but also locks up a substantial portion of the meagre
capital of the small industrialist. The industrial estate has been
envisaged as an effective means by which the small industrialist
can save his effort, time and capital in setting up a factory.

An estate is an attempt to provide, on a rental basis, good
accommodation and other basic common facilities to groups of
small enterpreneurs who would otherwise find it difficult to
secure these facilities at a reasonable price. These facilities are
expected to be provided economically at an estate because of
the operation of economies of scale in the construction of a large
number of factories. The estate also makes possible the setting
up of common technical, workshop, repair and other services,
which would not pay for one small factory alone but may pay
for a number of them. This is the economic rationale for setting up industrial estates.

The industrial estate has been used as a mechanism to stimulate the growth and efficiency of small industries in the U. K.,
U. S. A., Holland and elsewhere. Industrial estates—or trading
estates—were first started in the U. K. before World War II to
divert industry into what were called "depressed" or "distressed"
areas, i. e. areas of heavy unemployment. The success of the
estates in the U. K. induced the Small Scale Industries Board to
suggest to the Government of India to use the estate as a means
of promoting the planned growth of small industries. This was
towards the end of the First Plan, and the programme got under
way during the Second Plan.

The Second Plan defined the 'principal objective' of these
estates as follows : "to enable a number of small scale units to

35

have the advantage of common services and other facilities, such as a good site, electricity, water, gas, steam, compressed air, railway siding, watch and ward, etc." Since, in an industrial estate, a number of manufacturing establishments are located within the same area, it was also expected that an estate would, in effect, become a complex of interdependent and interrelated industries. Such a complex is expected to have the advantages of agglomeration and external economies which are necessary for the growth of individual industrial units.

With the development of plans for small industries, the Government aims regarding industrial estates have also been further broadened. The estates are expected to :

   (i) relieve the existing congestion in industrial areas and big towns and thus serve as a tool of city planning ;

  (ii) stimulate growth of small industries in the townships surrounding some major industrial plants and thus promote growth of auxiliary industries ;

 (iii) decentralise industry towards small towns and large villages and thus control urban growth and regulate location of industries.

To enable the estates to implement these objectives, all the prevailing methods of assistance devised for the promotion of small-scale industries, such as technical advice, marketing aids, financial assistance, greater availability of raw materials and power, etc., are combined. The application of these developmental measures for small industries is organisationally easier in the estates where small enterprises are concentrated. A study of the industrial estates thus provides an opportunity of examining the many-sided aid programme of the Government for small industries as a sort of "controlled experiment".

The data collected and presented in this section are partly based on published materials and partly on the results of field research. The authors interviewed a number of Government officials in charge of the programme and also visited a number of estates.[1] In the course of their visits, the authors had discussions with State Directors of Industries, and officials in charge of the estates, as well as a fairly large number of operating entrepreneurs. Two sorts of schedules were distribu-

---

[1] Ludhiana (Punjab), Okhla (Delhi), Sanatnagar (Andhra), Guindy and Madurai (Madras), Pappanamcode and Ettumanoor (Kerala).

ted : a general schedule requesting information for the estate as a whole, to be filled in by the administration : and a factory schedule to be filled in by the individual entrepreneur, giving information about the operation of the individual factory. Out of 34 functioning estates, general schedules were returned for only 12. These estates contain 206 factories. Of the 483 factories operating in all functioning estates, factory schedules were collected in respect of 126 factories. Though the data lack complete coverage they give some insight into the situation in estates in the different parts of the country. The data presented in the statistical tables do not always refer to the same number of factories, partly because some of the schedules received were incomplete and partly because some information sought in the schedule became available from other sources as well. It should also be remembered that the position in the estates is changing continually. The figures given below refer to the position obtaining in the early months of 1960.

PROGRESS IN THE CONSTRUCTION OF ESTATES

As the programme of industrial estate was accepted by the Government of India in 1955, only ten estates were sanctioned for the First Plan. Out of these, one was partially completed (at Rajkot) and construction of the rest was carried over to the Second Plan. The Second Plan originally envisaged the building of 100 new industrial estates but on a reappraisal of the Plan, the programme was reduced to 87 estates. Thus 97 estates have so far been sanctioned of which 20 are rural estates and 9 are in the pilot project areas. For this programme alloactions under the First and Second Plans have totalled about Rs. 12 crores.

The Government of India advances the cost of constructing estates in the form of loans. The cost of preliminary planning and preparation of layout is treated as a grant. But the responsibility for the construction and management of the estates rests with the State Governments. In the beginning, when there was no model of industrial estates in the country, the construction and management of two estates (Okhla and Naini) were given to the National Small Industries Corporation on a pilot basis.[2]

[2] The Okhla estate has since been handed over to the Delhi Administration.

Practically all the States have undertaken the construction work and management of the estates through their own Industries Departments. Bombay alone has made arrangements to construct estates by advancing loans to municipalities, co-operative societies and registered companies.

TABLE 8

PROGRESS OF THE ESTATES PROGRAMME

	1955-56	56-57	57-58	58-59	59-60	Total
Number of estates sanctioned	10	13	43	20	11	97
Number of estates which started functioning[a]	1	...	10	20	3	34
Advances to State Governments and N.S.I.C. (lakhs of rupees)						
Grants	0.5	0.4	0.7	Nil	Nil	1.6
Loans	58.0	110.8	193.0	199.1	241.7	802.6
Amount spent by State Governments and N.S.I.C. (lakhs of rupees)	12.5	96.4	211.4	218.7	259.3	798.3

[a] A "functioning" estate does not necessarily mean that all the factory sheds have been occupied. It means an estate where a sizeable number of factories have started working.

The progress of the programme can be seen from Table 8. The final column shows the situation reached by January 1960. Since then 5 more estates have started functioning. Besides, 10 other estates are ready and are likely to start functioning in the near future. Another 9 are nearing completion. By the end of the Second Plan it is hoped that about 60 estates will be functioning in different parts of the country.[3]

Thus, progress in the construction of industrial estates has fallen somewhat behind schedule. The principal reason for this has been the time-consuming processes involved in the acquisition of land and the delays caused by the P. W. D. According to the Sub-Committee on Industrial Estates "a period of two years has been taken in acquiring land, making plans and estimates and starting construction of the estates".[4] The Selected

[3] cf. *Third Five Year Plan—a Draft Outline.*
[4] *Report of the Sub-Committee on Industrial Estates, p. 15.*

Buildings Project Team, which reported on Industrial Estates, noted that one set of factories which were to be completed in $5\frac{1}{2}$ months actually took $13\frac{1}{2}$ months, although "steel construction was justified on grounds of shortage of time."[5] In the estates covered in this study the construction of an estate has taken from 7 to 22 months from the beginning of ground clearance to the start of work by the *first* factory.

On the basis of experience so far, it cannot be said that the gestation period of small enterprises in industrial estates is significantly less than that of large-scale enterprises. But this time-lag does not, of course, tie up the finances of the private entrepreneur, who moves in only when the factory and other facilities are ready.

The following table summarises the data on the utilisation of sheds in the 34 estates which had started functioning in early 1960 :

TABLE 9

POSITION REACHED BY EARLY 1960

Number of sheds completed	1,051
Number of sheds allotted	942
Number of factories working[a]	483
Average number of persons employed per factory[b]	19
Total annual gross product[c]	Rs. 7.3 crores
Total number of persons employed[c]	9,200

[a] Some factories use more than one shed, and some sheds are used by the Government.

[b] Estimate based on 252 factories for which relevant data were available from the office of the Development Commissioner, Small-Scale Industries, New Delhi.

[c] Estimate for 483 factories blown up from sample of 252 factories.

LOCATION AND SITING OF ESTATES

Most of the functioning estates are situated near cities or big towns. In Kerala, however, four out of six estates are located near medium towns. All the estates are on trunk or branch roads and near railway stations or sidings.

[5] *Report of the Selected Buildings Project Team*, p. 27.

The table below briefly summarises the locational pattern of the estates for which data are available.

TABLE 10

PATTERN OF LOCATION

Name of estate	Name of nearest town	Distance from nearest town (miles)	1951 population of nearest town (in lakhs)	Distance from nearest railway station (miles)
Okhla	Delhi	7	13.8	$\frac{3}{4}$
Ludhiana	Ludhiana	$1\frac{1}{2}$	1.5	1
Naini	Allahabad	7	3.3	$\frac{1}{2}$ (siding)
Sanatnagar	Hyderabad	7	10.9	$\frac{3}{8}$
Cuttack	Cuttack	—	1.0	—
Guindy	Madras	7	14.2	$\frac{1}{4}$
Madurai	Madurai	3	3.6	$1\frac{1}{2}$
Pappanamcode	Trivandrum	$4\frac{1}{2}$	1.8	4
Kollakadavu	Alleppey	—	1.2	2-3 (proposed)
Ettumanoor	Kottayam	6	0.4	$1\frac{1}{2}$
Ollur	Trichur	$4\frac{1}{2}$	0.7	$\frac{1}{2}$
Olavakkot	Palghat	6	0.7	—

Most of the estates already functioning are urban estates. The rural estates were intended to be located near very small towns or big villages, but many of these estates have not been constructed so far. There is only one such estate actually functioning—at Marathandam.[6] It has 5 completed sheds of which 4 have been allotted ; but regular production has started in one unit only. Noting this fact, the Working Group on the Programme of Work for the Third Plan complained that the estates have not "succeeded to any perceptible degree in establishing small-scale industries in underdeveloped areas, which was also one of the important objectives of the Government in starting industrial estates."[7] The Estimates Committee of the Lok Sabha in their Report on Small Scale Industries have also pointed out that "one of the major criteria for setting up the estimates viz., decentralisation of industrial development remains unfulfilled."[8]

[6] Two more have ben constructed at Bihar Shariff (Bihar) and Dhekiajuli (Assam) but they have not started functioning yet.

[7] Report of the Working Group, p. 67.

[8] 7th Report of the Estimates Committee, Part I, p. 26.

The basis for these complaints seems to be the *a priori* assumption that the scheme of industrial estates is an effective instrument for decentralisation. This assumption has been examined in the previous seçtion. Here it might be pointed out that the Working Group itself does not appear to have either made a case for such estates or worked out the way to go about bringing them into existence. They maintain that "considerations like proximity to markets, particularly in regard to consumer industries, nearness to equipment and machinery for repairing and service workshops, availability of technical know-how and skilled workers, and essential facilities like transport, water, power, etc. influenced location of small scale units in cities and towns. Such of the small scale units as have to be developed as ancillaries to large scale factories had necessarily to be located near the parent units which were invariably in towns."[9] Then, without any more argument, they suggest that "these considerations will *obviously* have to be given less importance if the objective of taking industries to rural areas is to be fulfilled more effectively. (Italics ours). After stating the objective, they merely enunciate that the estates as "one of the effective instruments for dispersal of industries should be more actively fostered during the Third Plan period."[10] This is immediately followed by a counsel of caution emphasising that "due consideration will have to be paid to various factors like entrepreneurial talent in rural areas."[11] These statements illustrate the current state of confusion about the role of industrial estates and their potentialities.

The nature of the enterprises that will operate in rural industrial estates has not been defined. It appears that these estates will be smaller versions of the existing industrial estates. The sort of enterprises that are operating in the estates are modern small mechanised factories. For the success of such secondary manufacturing industry the existence of a large number of social and economic overheads is necessary. Apart from the existence of infra-structure, like transport and power, skilled labour must also be available. There should also be marketing facilities nearby through which the products can be sold. Above all,

[9] *Report of the Working Group*, p. 69.
[10] Ibid., pp. 67-68.
[11] Ibid., pp. 69.

entrepreneurs who are willing and capable of taking advantage of the factory sheds and other facilities must also be available. In the absence of these prerequisites the idea of rural industrial estates appears to be somewhat premature.

Even the proximity of a large or medium town does not necessarily guarantee the success of an estate. There are cases where difficulties have arisen because of the absence of some crucial prerequisite for industrial growth. Naini is an outstanding example of this. Similarly, entrepreneurs in Kollakadavu estate near Alleppey in Kerala are facing difficulties in marketing their products in the neighbouring areas. Thus, while the existence of infra-structure is a necessary—but not a sufficient—condition for the success of an industrial estate, availability of enterprise is the key factor. This may be illustrated with reference to the industrial estates at Ludhiana and Naini.

In Ludhiana estate, there is no difficulty in finding applicants for factories, even at unsubsidised rents. Before the last war, Ludhiana was a centre of hosiery manufacture, and this is still its largest single industry, employing about 8,000 persons. But during the war, and particularly after the influx of refugees from West Pakistan in 1947, there was a significant growth in engineering industries like bicycles and bicycle parts. sewing machines, automobile parts, machinery and machine tools.

Apart from these factories which are located in the industrial areas, thousands of small workshops and factories are to be found scattered all over the town. Badly lighted workshops, each containing about half a dozen workers, can be seen in practically all parts of the town, turning out various assortments of products. Nevertheless, they manage to make fairly good products which enjoy large and widespread markets. The defects of their products are mostly due to the shortage of standard raw materials rather than to inferior quality of workmanship.

With such a plenitude of enterprise and skills available the success of the industrial estate at Ludhiana was a foregone conclusion. The shortage of factory space is chronic, and it would require several industrial estates put together to relieve the congestion in the town. The crucial limiting factor in the growth and multiplication of small industries in Ludhiana and other Punjab towns is shortage of power and the required raw materials. The industrial estate itself cannot solve these problems, except for those individual factories which manage to get into the estate.

The Ludhiana estate occupies a plot of land in one of the two industrial areas developed by the Government. In these industrial areas, plots have been rented or sold to entrepreneurs on which they have put up their own buildings. The estate can be distinguished from the surrounding factories by the greater standardisation of its buildings. It is utilitarian in appearance and is built in an economical style. Of the 52 factory sheds completed so far, one is used as a canteen, 5 are temporarily used for administrative purposes (of which only one is used for the administration of the estate itself), and the remaining 46 are occupied by private firms. A further 108 sheds are now being built. A simple administrative block will eventually be provided.

In contrast to Ludhiana estate stands the one at Naini. Naini is situated at a distance of 7 miles from Allahabad. The estate was set up in this area because there is no land closer to the city which is at the same time high enough to escape the floods of the Ganges and the Jamuna. The first phase of the programme of construction was over in January 1959, when 40 factory sheds (along with the usual complement of common services) were completed. These services included a water tank, a power-house and a railway siding. Allahabad is a much larger town than Ludhiana, but it is primarily an administrative, trading and pilgrim centre. It is also a university town. Unlike Ludhiana, Allahabad does not have any large industry, nor does it have a sizeable small industry. For instance, in basic metal industries and metal products it had in 1956 only two medium-sized factories and half a dozen repair workshops.[12] There were, therefore, no entrepreneurs in Allahabad straining at the leash, anxious to move out to better accommodation where their activities would not be cramped for lack of space or where the existence of common facilities would help them to multiply their product.

In January 1960, only 4 factories were in operation in Naini, employing 87 persons and producing products of the gross value of Rs. 1,15,000. At that time only 9 sheds had been occupied and even the occupants of these did not pay the rent of 8 n. p.

[12] Source : *Large Industrial Establishments in India, 1956.*

per square foot, which is one half of the economic rent.[13]   In short, Allahabad did not possess an industrial base from which the estate at Naini could be projected.

Ludhiana and Naini represent two limiting types of urban estates that have emerged so far.   Between these two types other estates can be fitted in in terms of their resemblance with the one or the other.   The Kerala estates, for example, are facing a paucity of local entrepreneurs.

TABLE 11

UTILISATION OF FACTORY SHEDS IN KERALA

Estate	No. of sheds completed	No. of sheds allotted to		Total allotted sheds	No. of allotted sheds unoccupied
		private entre-preneurs	Government establishments		
Pappanamcode	32	23	9	32	2
Kollakadavu	42	12	3	15	3
Ettumanoor	31	17	14	31	6
Ollur	42	27	6	33	11
Olavakkot	34	22	5	27	9
Palyad	11	4	—	4	—
TOTAL	192	105	37	142	31
(Percentage)	(100)	(55)	(19)	(74)	(16)

As can be seen from Table 11, of all the sheds completed in Kerala estates only 55 per cent have so far been allotted to private entrepreneurs ; and 30 per cent of these have not so far been put to any use.

From our study of estates we can draw the following conclusions about location : (a) it is very difficult to establish successful estates in backward areas where the necessary infra-structure of communications, markets and financial facilities is lacking ; (b) some estates, which are situated in the neighbourhood of quite large towns, offering reasonable general facilities, have nevertheless been slow to develop because of a shortage of local entrepreneurs and skilled labour.

[13] Out of total rent of about Rs. 1,40,000 due at the end of March 1960, only a little over Rs. 11,000 had been paid.

We shall come back to the question of spreading industry in backward areas later, after we have reviewed the Government's efforts to create entrepreneurs.

The selection of a good site for an estate is as important as the selection of proper location. In view of the multiplicity of purposes which the industrial estates are expected to serve, the sites are not always chosen with a view to promoting the maximum efficiency of enterprises operating in the estates. "Some of the State Governments decided that an estate should be put up as far removed from the town as possible without considering the difficulties of providing the necessary facilities such as transport, housing of workers, availability of power, drainage, roads, water, etc."[14]

The selection of a site for an estate involves the difficult task of balancing engineering, economic, and other considerations. A site should have a topography which will permit easy drainage. It should be within easy reach of water and power sources. It should not be too far away from sources of labour and raw materials, markets for finished products and means of transport. If to these considerations are added those of city planning, slum clearance and local political pressures, the selection of sites becomes very difficult indeed. There should be no surprise, therefore, that certain sites have not proved to be ideal. For example, Cuttack complains of difficulties of drainage; Kollakadavu, of exposure to winds which damage the structures and result in stoppage of work; Naini, of difficulties of getting labour from Allahabad and so forth. An inconvenient site always results finally in the need for more investment. Very often the distance from the town increases either the wage costs of the factories in the estate or Government investment in labour housing.

The policy of setting up estates at long distances from their neighbouring towns seems, sometimes, to be mistaken for a policy of decentralisation of industry. The problem of decentralisation is a problem of location and not of siting. It would be an odd kind of decentralisation which merely resulted in estates being put as far away as possible from their associated towns.

[14] Report of the Sub-Committee on Industrial Estates, p. 15.

SIZE AND TYPES OF FACTORIES

As was mentioned above, on the basis of the data available for 206 factories, the average number of persons employed in the factories already operating in the estates is about 19. But there is considerable variation in the sizes of the factories both within estates and between estates, as will be seen from Table 12. Almost half of the factories employ less than 10 workers ; about a third between 10 and 40 workers ; and the remaining one-sixth employ 40 or more. As time passes this picture is likely to change. Many factories have not gone into full production as yet, mainly because of shortage of raw materials. In Ludhiana, this has been further aggravated recently by shortage of power. With greater availability of raw materials and power, the size of the factories in the estates, particularly at Ludhiana, will tend to grow and approach nearer to the Okhla dimensions. It should be noted that the Okhla factories are significantly larger than those in the other estates.

TABLE 12

DISTRIBUTION OF FACTORIES BY DIFFERENT LABOUR SIZE GROUPS

Estate	Number of persons employed						Total no. of factories	Average no. of persons employed
	Under 10	10-19	20-29	30-39	40-49	50 & above		
Okhla	1	1	2	5	12	8	29	46
Ludhiana	35	9	—	—	2	—	46	9
Kanpur	8	4	—	—	—	1	13	17
Naini	3	2	—	1	4	—	10	21
Sanatnagar	11	6	2	—	—	2	21	16
Cuttack	4	12	—	—	—	1	17	16
Madurai	6	1	—	—	1	1	9	16
Pappanamcode	3	1	5	3	—	1	13	21
Kollakadavu	2	3	—	1	—	2	8	25
Ettumanoor	3	2	2	—	—	1	8	26
Ollur	14	5	—	—	1	—	20	9
Olavakkot	8	2	1	—	—	1	12	15
TOTAL	98	48	12	12	18	18	206	19

When selecting firms for entry into the estates, general preference has been shown for what are called "new industries", such as light engineering and some chemical industries. Many of these industries, especially in light engineering, grew up during the last war, but they have also been stimulated by the imposition of import restrictions in the more recent past. Hence, the majority of enterprises in the estates are modern small light engineering (mechanical and electrical) factories, producing a variety of fabricated consumer goods, machinery parts, tools, builders' hardware and so forth. One can expect that the larger the estate, the greater will be the diversity of these products and the larger the scope for intra-estate trade. So far, however, such trade had developed only in one or two large and diversified estates like Guindy in Madras.

Most of the products produced in the estates depend on standardised raw materials which are produced in large factories and have to come over long distances. Similarly, for the disposal of their products, these factories have to depend on markets much larger than 'local' markets. Many of these enterprises are directly in competition with larger enterprises, although such competition is not very much in evidence currently because of import restrictions and the non-expansion of larger enterprises in some industries.

Since the technique used in the manufacture of engineering products is modern, there is very little scope for these enterprises to be labour-intensive or capital-saving. This is borne out by the data presented in later paragraphs on the output-capital and capital-labour ratio of factories operating in the estates. For example, units which manufacture simple but modern products like wire nails, barbed wire, snap buttons or polythene bags use a few automatic machines. Larger firms making the same products would use similar equipment, but since they would have a larger scale of output they would probably make more effective use of their equipment.

There are, however, situations in which it is advantageous for the big firm to get some of its requirements like a component or a tool from a small subcontracting firm. Small firms may be able to produce such items more cheaply because of their lower overheads, lower wages, and more flexible production programme. A vertical disintegration of this sort creates flexibility in the industrial structure as a whole. If the larger firm changes its requirements it can drop the small firm, whereas it could not so easily shuttle off capacity created within itself. Of course, the small firm must then look for new customers; but this may be possible in a dynamic market.

The arrangement is not 'ideal', especially for the small firms themselves, but it is probably better than encouraging all big firms to be self-sufficient. It was expected that factories which produce parts and components for bicycles, sewing machines, radios and so forth would develop into ancillaries to larger enterprises. In fact, the products of most such factories feed mainly the 'spares' market which is sensitive to price but not particularly sensitive to quality.

The main obstacle to the development of small factories as ancillaries is that their products are frequently 'sub-standard', i. e. they do not come up to prescribed specifications. This is not always the fault of the small entrepreneurs but is caused by the shortage of good quality raw materials, and the absence of proper facilities for electroplating, heat-treatment, die-casting, machining and so forth. Facilities of this sort are being increasingly provided at industrial estates, and with the greater availability of raw materials the scope for ancillary industries will undoubtedly grow.

ATTEMPTS AT DEVELOPMENT OF "LATENT" ENTERPRISE

Much emphasis is placed on the aim of filling the industrial estates with "new" entrepreneurs. A "new" entrepreneur may be defined as one who was not previously running a *manufacturing* business. Many of those who start up in the estates have previously been in other kinds of business, especially trade.

Available data on the previous manufacturing connections of firms in the estates are given in Table 13.

A striking difference emerges here between the composition of Okhla firms and of the firms in the other estates. All but one of the 29 Okhla firms, for which data are available, had previously had a manufacturing business, outside the estate, while in the other estates only about one-third of the factories were allotted to firms already in manufacturing. Okhla, in other words, opened its doors to "going concerns" that needed better

TABLE 13

OLD AND NEW ENTERPRISES IN THE ESTATES

Estate	Total no. of firms	No. of firms previously owning outside factories	Percentage of col. 3 to col. 2	No. of firms retaining control of outside factories	Percentage of col. 5 to col. 3
1	2	3	4	5	6
Okhla	29	28	97	15	54
Ludhiana	46	17	37	1	6
Kanpur	13	5	38	N.A.	—
Naini	10	—	—	—	—
Sanatnagar	21	8	38	8	100
Cuttack	17	4	24	1	25
Madurai	9	3	33	N.A.	—
Pappanamcode	13	5	38	4	80
Kollakodavu	8	3	38	3	100
Ettumanoor	8	2	25	2	100
Ollur	20	5	25	3	60
Olavakkot	12	4	33	4	100
TOTAL	206	84	41	41	49

facilities for expansion, while the majority of firms in other estates were new recruits to manufacturing business. This difference helps to explain why the Okhla factories (as we saw in Table 12) are more than twice as large as the average for all estates. It also has a bearing on the economic results achieved by the factories in Okhla, which will be considered below.

Another interesting point to be noticed in Table 13 is that of the 17 factories in Ludhiana which were previously in manufacturing only one has retained control of its old business. This contrasts with the position in other estates, where most of the "old" manufacturers have kept a connection with their outside business. This may be explained by the fact that most of the Ludhiana estate factories are very small in terms of numbers employed (see Table 12). It seems that the firms recruited for the Ludhiana estate were nearly all either "new" manufacturers or very small firms which transferred their whole interests to the estate. In other estates, on the other hand, the "old" manufacturers which were brought in were generally larger firms which were, in effect, establishing branches within the estate. In such cases the expansion of the firm often results in diversification and division of labour between the old and the new establishments.

In the States where entrepreneurs have not been available in adequate numbers the Government has tried in several ways to create them. For instance, in Kerala, great efforts were made by the administration to induce an agriculturist to take to manufacturing, even to the extent of guaranteeing his market by securing a contract with a Government factory. In a situation like this, where entrepreneurs are not easily available and have to be coaxed into the estate, the administration has to take on the major portion of the entrepreneurial activity. And since the newly created entrepreneurs are usually not very enterprising, they are helped to set up units where the manufacturing of a product is very simple and the product in question is in short supply, such as wire nails ,barbed wire, snap buttons or polythene bags.

Another form of enterprise fostered by the Government is industrial cooperatives. These cooperatives are mostly conversions of former training-cum-production centres which qualify for additional assistance by virtue of their becoming cooperatives. They are mainly run by Government-paid managers, and, to enable the members to contribute to the share capital, financial assistance is also provided by the Government. The Government also helps in marketing. For example, a cooperative at Pappanamcode produces file boards and covers for the Kerala Government offices. Sometimes a firm which has not made good becomes a cooperative society. In Kerala, again, there is a radio-assembling cooperative which started as a partnership and, after not doing well for a period, was converted into a cooperative. It is still not doing well; but now it has Government support.

Some State Governments have decided to make it easy for private enterprise to function by taking it upon themselves to start a factory as a public project with the aim of selling it eventually to a small businessman, once the project has proved successful. The principle behind this programme is difficult to understand. If one believes that private enterprise is really enterprising, and that it can play an important role in develop-

ing the economy, then it is illogical to expect the Government
to undertake all the real risk-taking and organisation, with the
private "entrepreneur" coming in only when the business is a
going concern. It is significant, however, that none of these projects has yet got to the point of becoming saleable.

Finally, the Government also steps in as an entrepreneur in its
own right. For example at Pappanamcode, the Government has
4 small factories of its own, producing cycles, leather footwear,
small machine tools and lenses and precision instruments. The
cycle unit was started as a Government private limited concern
but, after running into difficulties, it has now been taken over
by the Department of Industries to be run departmentally. This
factory has never gone into full production for one reason or
another.

In general, these direct efforts to create and foster private
enterprise have not been very successful. If the Government's
intervention as an entrepreneur is found to be necessary it seems
to us that it would be better for it to concentrate its efforts and
resources in large public sector projects, locating them so far as
possible in industrially backward areas. This would also, in
fact, be a more promising method of stimulating the development of small entrepreneurs in these areas. Large factories have
often been the breeding ground for potential entrepreneurs. In
them skilled workers acquire knowledge of techniques and production processes, and the more ambitious among them, given
possibilities of commercial success, branch out and set up their
own enterprises. One of the most successful entrepreneurs at
Sanatnagar (producing steel furniture) is a former employee of
a nearby large factory. At Guindy, three former industrial
engineers have combined to manufacture gears, industrial gear
boxes and gear pumps. Their factory is doing well and has
plans to expand to cope with increasing orders. At Madurai,
a former technician of a well-known firm of automobile body-
builders has taken a shed in the estate to manufacture garage
tools, which are in short supply in the country.

THE ENTREPRENEURS' ATTITUDES TO THE ESTATES

In the factory schedules a question was asked about the reasons that attracted the entrepreneurs to the estates. Most of the

entrepreneurs conceded that it had been an advantage to them to move to ready-made factories, thereby reducing their gestation period and the investment requirements for fixed assets. But many of them would not have entered the estates solely because of the availability of rental buildings. Some of them could have raised the finance for buildings on their own. Others wanted to buy their factory sheds and pay for them on an instalment basis. Many would be prepared to set up their own factories if a developed area were earmarked for this purpose.

There are a great many complaints about the rents, even though in all but one of the estates the rents paid are only half the economic rent. Out of 126 entrepreneurs who filled up factory schedules, as many as 95 considered existing rents high. It is possible that this opinion was only a tactic to resist the full economic rent from being charged. The subsidy on rent, however, is not regarded by the entrepreneurs as an assistance to them. They regard it as the price which the Government must pay for their high costs of construction and lavishness of layout. This has also been the opinion of the Committee on Plan Projects which examined the estates projects from this point of view. They suggested ways and means of reducing the capital costs of construction, maintaining that the "answer to low rent is lower cost of construction and not higher subsidy".

A few of the entrepreneurs mentioned financial assistance as an inducement for entering the estate. That there is an advantage on this score is indicated by some comparative figures collected for the Okhla estate and for outside firms also operating in Delhi.[15] These show that out of their total financial requirements, the Okhla factories received about 11 per cent directly from the Government or from the National Small Industries Corporation, whereas outside factories received less than 3 per cent from these sources. In addition, of course, the Okhla factories were relieved of the necessity of finding capital for their buildings.

But the dominant attraction of the industrial estates so far has been the guarantee of power and raw materials, and a more favoured treatment in the grant of import licences. By becoming the Government's tenant the entrepreneur in an estate is able to get over a number of hurdles in one jump. So long as short-

---

[15] The figures were assembled by the Development Commissioner, Small Scale Industries.

ages of power and raw materials continue, so long will the demand for industrial estates be inflated, particularly in areas where enterprise and skills are available.

In some estates the entrepreneurs are not yet getting sufficient power and raw materials. For example, 35 out of 39 entrepreneurs of the Ludhiana estate complain of shortage of power. Similarly, 79 out of 117 entrepreneurs of different estates complain of shortage of raw materials. One of the common suggestions made at different estates is to set up raw material depots for supplying estate factories.

In spite of these difficulties, however, the entrepreneurs in the estates are generally better off in respect of both power and raw materials than those outside. It must be recognised that an improvement in the position of factories inside the estates may merely aggravate the raw materials shortage for factories outside the estates. According to an informed guess about a northern estate, the 'outside' factories are able to get only 15 to 20 per cent of their raw materials requirements at controlled prices, the rest of their supplies being derived from the 'open market'. This sort of situation represents a concealed subsidy for the factories in the estates, either in the form of a price advantage in raw materials or in the form of a redistribution of capacity utilisation in their favour.

The clamour for estates is not, therefore, necessarily an index of the success of the estates as such. It may be merely an index of the intensity of the shortages of raw materials and power.

THE RELATIONS OF CAPITAL, LABOUR AND OUTPUT IN THE ESTATES

In view of the argument that small enterprises are labour-using and capital-saving, it is interesting to study the output-capital and capital-labour ratios of the factories operating in the estates and compare them with the figures given in the previous section of this paper.

Capital here has been computed as the sum of replacement cost of machinery, the cost of land and buildings provided by the estate and the value of stocks.[16] By output is meant annual net

[16] The value of land and buildings for the factories for which ratios have been calculated were estimated by apportioning to them the capital expenditure of the estate on a pro-rata basis.

value added by manufacture. By labour is meant all persons engaged in the factory including working proprietors. Table 14 summarises the results.

TABLE 14

OUTPUT-CAPITAL AND CAPITAL-LABOUR RATIOS IN ESTATE FACTORIES[a]

Estate	Average No. of persons employed per factory	Output per unit of capital	Output per person employed (Rs.)	Capital per person employed (Rs.)
1	2	3	4	5
Okhla	46	0.41	2535	6341
Ludhiana[b]	9	0.21	1973	7807
Sanatnagar	21	0.27	3199	12479
Kerala estates	17	0.15	1069	5074
TOTAL	19	0.31	2037	6992

[a] Because of incompleteness of data the figures in columns 3, 4 and 5 do not always relate to the same number of factories.

[b] In Ludhiana the value of stocks was not available. It has been imputed at the rate of 25% of annual gross value of output, which is the average for all the other estates taken together.

Several points have to be borne in mind before interpreting the data presented in the table. First, the output-capital and output-labour ratios for Ludhiana are underestimates. The data were collected when, owing to a temporary dislocation of the power system, electricity was rationed, and as a result the factories were closed for two days in a week. If allowance were made for this, the output-capital ratio for Ludhiana would rise to about 0.3 and output per person to nearly Rs. 3,000. Secondly, the figures for Sanatnagar are based on only five factories and, on this account, should not be taken too seriously. The very high capital-labour ratio is untypical of estate factories generally.

Subject to these qualifications, the figures give some indication of the position obtaining in industrial estates. They show that, even in Okhla, which is the oldest of this group and the one with the largest factories, the output-capital ratio has only attained 0.41. This is about the figure implicit in the "Model Schemes", after adjustment for below-capacity working; but it is not a particularly high figure by comparison with the results obtainable in larger factories (see Table 5). From a purely capital-saving point of view, therefore, it is difficult to justify the building of industrial estates.

In the other estates the situation is even less favourable. Ludhiana, as we have said, will show better results when it receives adequate power ; and it will also improve further as the small Ludhiana factories expand into their new premises. But it seems unlikely that the Ludhiana factories will do any better than Okhla. Sanatnagar may also show better results as time passes ; but the Kerala estates, which have been in existence for quite a long time, have a very poor performance.

One of the reasons for the low output-capital ratios in the estates (and the high capital-labour ratios) is the high cost of construction of the estates. According to our figures, the cost of land, buildings and other construction work at the estates represents about half the total capital per operating factory, the remaining half being investment in machinery and stocks.[17] A comparable estimate from the Model Schemes would show less than a third of the total capital invested in land and buildings.[18]

[17] The percentage share of Government investment to total investment works out for Okhla, Ludhiana, Sanatnagar and Kerala estates as 40, 61, 51, and 59 respectively. These figures have been computed as follows. Land and building costs per factory equal total cost of the estate divided by the number of factories on the estate. Other capital per factory equals total replacement cost of machinery plus value of stocks divided by the number of factories for which this information is available.

[18] The high cost of land, buildings, and other assets built by the Government in the estates have been noted by Governmental Committees which have examined this aspect of industrial estates. The pattern of layout, land utilisation, etc., varies widely from estate to estate. The result is that development costs vary within very wide limits, from a minimum of 50 nP. to Rs. 16 per sq. foot. See Report of the Sub-Committee on Industrial Estates, p. 16). Commenting on the construction of the Okhla estate, the Selected Buildings Project Team observed that "half the money has been spent on works other than the factory buildings. The area utilised for roads, open spaces and ancillary buildings is 64 per cent. With proper planning, it should have been possible to have increased the area under the plots to about 60 per cent. It is difficult to understand the necessity of a 150 ft. wide highway within the industrial estate. The money spent on the ancillary buildings could have been more usefully utilised on the factory buildings which, after

The Selected Buildings Project Team has now laid down norms and standards which are aimed at reducing the capital cost of the construction of estates. If these measures are applied, the average construction cost per factory should fall by about 20 per cent, which would reduce the total capital required by 10 per cent. Thus the expected output-capital ratio would rise and, for efficient factories, might attain about 0.45. Even this, however, is not as good as the results obtainable in large-scale enterprises, especially if they work more than one shift.

It may be suggested that estate factories might also be persuaded to go over to multi-shift working. But the small industrialist usually finds it difficult to run more than one shift because of managerial limitations. The small industrialist is usually unable or unwilling to delegate managerial tasks to non-relatives. The size of his enterprise often reaches its maximum limit when his own management ability is fully stretched out. This is what marks him off from the big entrepreneur and this is the principal reason for his unwillingness and inability to work for more than one shift. Of the 206 factories for which information was collected, only 25 worked two shifts. The second shift was usually run by another partner or some close relation like the proprietor's son or brother, and seldom by a hired manager. Thus more intensive use of capital by running multiple shifts does not appear to be feasible for the small factories of the estates.

The average amount of net value added by manufacture per worker per year in the different estates is shown in column 4 of Table 14 above. According to these figures, the net output per worker at Okhla and Ludhiana is two to two and a half times greater than in the Kerala estates. The higher figure for Sanatnagar is, again, not to be treated as typical for that estate.

Column 5 of Table 14 indicates the magnitude of capital requirements per person employed in the estates. The average amount of capital employed per person in the estates, barring Sanatnagar, is within the range of Rs. 5,000-8,000. This is high compared with the figure of about Rs. 2,000 per worker obtaining in the Delhi light engineering industries using power and employ-

all, is the essence of a project." (p. 27). The Okhla factories have fortunately mitigated, to a certain extent, these disadvantages by making fuller use of their factory space.

ing less than 20 persons.[19] This is partly due to the fact that the light engineering products of the estates are somewhat different from those covered in the Delhi survey and partly due to the high-cost spacious buildings of the estates. But at the same time it does indicate the more mechanised nature of techniques employed in the estate factories. The higher figure for Sanatnagar is mainly due to higher land and building and other costs of that estate. Okhla too has high land and building costs, but the fact that it has the largest number of factories working on two shifts brings down the level of its capital intensity to that of other estates.

EMPLOYMENT PROVIDED BY ESTATES

One of the principal motives for building industrial estates is the provision of employment. It is relevant, therefore, to consider how much extra employment has actually been created by them. This is not quite as easy a question to answer as may be thought at first.

It is simple enough, in principle, to collect figures on the actual number of persons employed on a given date. But if we want to know the *extra* employment provided by an estate, we should allow for the fact that some of the factories in it were already working before the estate was built. In that case the net additional employment by the firms in the estate would be measured by the number employed now, minus the number employed before transferring to the estate, plus the number *still* employed in outside factories which are still owned by the firms. Figures of this sort were collected for 121 factories in 8 estates, and the results are shown in Table 15.

Total employment in these estates was 2,912 or an average of 24 per factory, of which 2,303 or 19 per factory represented net additional employment. Since the position in Okhla is untypical it may be better to exclude that estate in estimating the averages. In that case, average total employment per factory becomes 17.3, of which net additional employment is 16.2. If we apply this last figure to the 454 factories in estates other than

[19] This figure of Rs. 2,000 is estimated after making allowance for land and buildings and stocks of finished goods. The Delhi survey gives a figure of Rs. 1,500, exclusive of these components.

TABLE 15

NET ADDITION TO EMPLOYMENT

Estate	No. of factories	Employment in the outside business		Employment in the estates	Net addition to employment (4+5 — 3)	Percentage of col. 6 to col. 5
		Previously	Currently			
(1)	(2)	(3)	(4)	(5)	(6)	(7)
Okhla	29	1012	511	1321	820	63
Naini	11	Nil	Nil	212	212	100
Sanatnagar	21	363	345	334	316	95
Pappanamcode	13	318	278	276	236	86
Kollakadavu	8	210	200	200	190	95
Ettumanoor	7	105	105	207	207	100
Ollur	20	275	247	183	155	85
Olavakkot	12	220	208	179	167	93
TOTAL above	121	2503	1894	2912	2303	79
TOTAL (excluding Okhla)	92	1491	1383	1591	1483	93

Okhla, and then add back the Okhla figures, we arrive at an estimated net additional employment in the 34 estates now functioning (mid-1960) of nearly 8,200. This figure, however, does not allow for the possible continued use of premises outside the estates which previously were used by firms now in the estates, but which were not kept on by those firms (or their associates) after moving into the estate. If all these old factories continued to operate—under new management—and to employ the same number of people as before, the additional employment generated by the estates would be equal to their present *actual* employment. On this basis the additional employment given by the 34 estates can be estimated at nearly 9,200.[20]

Even this, however, does not tell us what the *ultimate* employment in these estates will be. A large number of factories in the estates, especially in the more backward areas, are not being used to their full capacity. The extent of underutilisation will be seen from Table 16 which has been computed on the basis of the relevant data received from 87 factories out of 126 surveyed.

[20] 454×17.3 plus, 1,321 for Okhla. This figure checks with the estimate shown in Table 9 which was derived by a different method and based on a larger sample of factories.

TABLE 16

DISTRIBUTION OF FACTORIES ACCORDING TO THE DEGREE OF UNDERUTILISATION OF CAPACITY

Percentage of unutilised capacity to total annual capacity[a]	Okhla	Ludhiana	Sanatnagar	Kerala estates	Total
Nil	6	2	1	15	24
1-10	—	—	—	—	—
11-20	2	—	1	1	4
21-30	3	1	—	2	6
31-40	6	1	1	5	13
41-50	2	6	1	2	11
51-60	3	5	—	3	11
61-70	—	6	—	—	7
71-80	1	—	—	2	3
81-90	—	2	—	2	4
91 & above	—	3	1	—	4
Total	24	26	5	32	87

[a] Annual capacity on the basis of a single shift.

It will be seen that 40 out of 87 factories have underutilised capacity ranging from 41 to over 90 per cent of their installed capacity. This is partly the result of the policy of filling the estates mainly with new firms, which take a long time to settle in, acquire raw materials, develop a market, and so on. It is impossible to say what the ultimate volume of employment given by the present estates will be, or how long it will take to reach that level, but a reasonable guess might be about 13,000.

An addition to employment—up to the present—of less than 10,000 seems, on the face of it, a rather disappointing result of five years of effort and the expenditure of more than Rs. 8 crores of Government money. This is partly a reflection of the time taken to get the programme started and of the many delays in carrying it out. It may be hoped that the future estates will be built more quickly. But even so, it seems that more attention should be given to the importance of achieving full utilisation of the factory sheds once they are completed. Some sheds stand idle for months on end for one reason or another, and the majority of them are underutilised, even after the factories have started working. The aim of full utilisation (and hence the creation of the maximum employment) can only be achieved if less emphasis is placed on trying to find entirely "new" and inexperienced entrepreneurs.

CONTRIBUTION OF ESTATES TO EMPLOYMENT IN THE THIRD PLAN

On the basis of the existing data on employment and investment in industrial estates so far, it is possible to give some rough idea of the magnitude of employment likely to be created by the estates in the course of the Third Plan.

The precise programme for industrial estates for the Third Plan is not known as yet. The Working Group set up by the Small Scale Industries Board has recommended a programme which involves a total Governmental outlay of about Rs. 50 crores. The Minister for Industries has, in a public statement, mentioned that the outlay will be of the order of Rs. 27 crores. If we assume that the Minister's figure of proposed Governmental outlay in industrial estates for the Third Plan is the final one, the gross additional employment created by the programme may be of the order of 98,000 and the net addition 91,000. These estimates are calculated as follows :

1. Value of estates to be completed during the Plan   Rs. 25 crores[a]

2. Estate cost per person employed :
   (a) at existing rates   Rs. 3,200[b]
   (b) allowing for 20 per cent economy in construction costs   Rs. 2,560[c]

3. Gross additional employment created   98,000[d]

4. Net additional employment created   91,000[e]

[a] Out of Rs. 27 crores actually spent it is assumed that Rs. 2 crores will represent an addition to the value of work in progress on uncompleted estates.

[b] Average figure for Okhla, Ludhiana and Kerala.

[c] Assuming that the norms laid down by the Selected Buildings Project Team are achieved.

[d] Line 1 divided by line 2(b).

[e] Assuming that only 93 per cent of gross employment is net, as in Table 15.

If we allow for a gradual increase during the Third Plan in the number of persons employed by the estates completed during the Second Plan, it seems that the total increase in employment in all estates during the Third Plan may be of the order of 100,000. This is not an inconsiderable number, but its achievement will depend very much on speed in carrying out the programme at all stages and on filling up the completed factories. In relation to the total demand for new jobs—an additional 14 million in the labour force plus a large backlog of unemployment—this programme in itself can make only a small contribution. Hence, it is all the more important that the firms selected for admittance to the industrial estates should be those with the maximum growth potential.

CONCLUSIONS

The main points that emerge out of the foregoing review of the Indian experiment in industrial estates are:

(1) The factories in industrial estates are small factories, which use power and modern machinery, and produce products for direct consumption or parts and components for other industries. These factories are the consequence of the recent developments in the country resulting in import restrictions, rise in national income, growth of modern transport and so forth.

(2) Industrial estates are designed to encourage the growth of small enterprises by providing the means by which small enterprises can capture the external economies of agglomeration. This economic rationale for industrial estates is sound. But the conditions precedent to such a development are the availability of enterprise and skills in the area where an estate is to be located. Such enterprise and skills are available only in areas where some industrial development has already taken place. In areas where such enterprises and skills are not available, industrial estates are not easily successful. The experience of such estates makes one doubt the effectiveness of estates as a method of spreading industry to non-industrial areas. If such areas are to develop industrially, it looks as if they must first have large industry. Small industry is a follower rather than a pioneer. Large industry will create external economies of agglomeration

as well as provide potential entrepreneurs from amongst the ranks of its skilled workers.

(3) The siting of estates has an important bearing on the efficiency and success of its factories. A wrong site results in heavier investment and heavier current costs of production. Technical and economic considerations should be given greater weight in the choosing of sites than the consideration for so-called dispersal of industry.

(4) The capital costs of construction of existing estates have been excessive. These excessive overheads have given some justification for the subsidising of rents. But unsubsidised rents can be paid by the entrepreneurs if the costs of construction are brought down and if more land is utilised for factories than has been the practice so far.

(5) Industrial estates can improve the technical efficiency and the chances of commercial success of small enterprises if they are large enough to be able to provide common technical and other facilities. In small estates the provision of such facilities is uneconomic because they remain largely underutilised.

(6) The techniques used in the factories in the estates are modern and mechanised. They are not labour-using and capital-saving, and they do not, therefore, create larger employment opportunities than could be had from medium or large factories making the same products. The justification for the estates is rather that they provide nursery beds in which efficient small entrepreneurs can grow. If this object were kept more firmly in mind there would be less waste of effort in trying to create "new" entrepreneurs and in offering valuable new facilities to people who are unable to make good use of them.

CHAPTER IV

OTHER PROGRAMMES FOR ASSISTING SMALL ENTERPRISES

THE Indian Government's programmes of assistance to small-scale enterprises are many-sided. In addition to the industrial estates programme—which we have just reviewed—there are provisions for giving technical, financial and marketing assistance to small firms, for the training of skilled workers, and for a variety of other purposes. The Japanese delegation which visited India in 1959 were so impressed by the comprehensiveness of these programmes that they wrote :

Speaking fairly and frankly, the small-scale industry policy of India is worked out with much scrupulousness in various phases. We dare say few counterparts can be found in the world in the number of items and in the elaborateness of their contents. In some aspects, we were first surprised to find that the policy was made up of a larger variety of measures than its Japanese counterpart which, we boast, goes ahead in the world.[1]

In this section we briefly review the various programmes of assistance now in operation—as well as some which have recently been proposed—to see how far they fulfill the objectives laid down earlier in this paper. As stated previously, the discussion will be limited to programmes designed to assist the development of modern small enterprises, which fall within the scope of the Small Scale Industries Board.

THE ORGANISATIONAL STRUCTURE

The development of small "industries" is, strictly speaking, a State subject, the primary responsibility for which rests with

---

[1] *Report of the Japanese Delegation on Small Scale Industries,* Ministry of Commerce and Industry, 1959. This was not, however, their final judgement on the policy. Within the limits of the courtesy to be expected from the official delegation, they expressed obvious concern about a tendency to overdo the amount of assistance given to small firms in India.

the State Directors of Industries. But, in recent years, two important central agencies have been established in order to give more impetus to the work. The first of these is the Central Small Industries Organisation, which is an administrative department—headed by a Development Commissioner—under the direct control of the Ministry of Commerce and Industry. Its primary responsibilities are to provide technical and marketing advice, which it organises through a number of Small Industries Service Institutes and Extension Centres. (There are at present 19 Institutes and 32 Extension Centres in various parts of the country.) The other central agency is the National Small Industries Corporation, which has been given various jobs. It has been made responsible for the promotion of schemes for supplying raw materials and components to small enterprises, for marketing their products, and also for the building of two of the industrial estates; but its most effective contribution, so far, has been in providing hire-purchase facilities for the supply of machinery to small firms. In the financial field a number of other agencies are at work, including the State Governments themselves, the State Finance Corporations, the Reserve Bank of India, the State Bank of India and the Cooperative Banks. Ultimate coordination of policy and function, between the various national agencies and the State Governments, is provided by the Small Scale Industries Board, on which all the bodies concerned are represented.

Inevitably, in view of the large number of different agencies at work in this field, there is some duplication of effort. For example, in some industrial estates common facility workshops have been provided both by the Central Small Industries Organisation and by the State Government. The proliferation of agencies and authorities also leads to tiresome administrative delays. For example, a small businessman wishing to set up a new enterprise which requires imported machinery had, at least until recently, to obtain the sanction, first, of the State Director of Industries, secondly, of the local Small Industries Service Institute and finally of the National Small Industries Corporatoin. Steps are now being taken to simplify some of these formalities. In the financial field, an important development has been the gradual spread of the "pilot" scheme of the State Bank of India, the object of which is to enable the entrepreneur to obtain from a single agency (the State Bank) advice on all the types of credit available to him.

The ultimate intention is that the various agencies giving assistance to small enterprises should be controlled by the States. This will certainly help to simplify coordination and eliminate the need for referring decisions from one level to another ; but as things stand at the present time there is no doubt that the small industries programme derives substantial benefits from the drive (and finance) which is being put into it from the Centre. And even in the ultimate situation, when the States have taken over full responsibility for the programme, there will still be room for some important functions to be carried out centrally, especially the pooling and publication of statistics, the provision of a clearing house of technical and marketing information, and the training of staff to work inside the organisation.

We shall now consider each of the main forms of assistance being provided to small-scale enterprises in India. They will be taken under the following six headings : technical assistance, financial assistance, marketing assistance, training of workers, provision of raw materials and power, and advice on the starting of new enterprises. In some cases several different agencies are concerned with the provision of a particular type of assistance. We shall mention these agencies in passing, but our main concern will be with the appropriateness of each programme rather than with the organisational arrangements for carrying it out.

TECHNICAL ASSISTANCE

Since the majority of small entrepreneurs have an insufficient technical and managerial background, and since private agencies for remedying these deficiencies are not able to meet the need, there is a good case for the Government to fill the breach. This case need not depend on any particular *preference* for small firms as such, but simply on the desirability of making existing enterprises more efficient than they are, so enabling some of them to expand into larger—and even more useful—enterprises. Technical advice is a type of aid which is least likely to be abused and most likely to be of social, as well as of purely private, benefit. Anybody can take a subsidy, or relax in the knowledge that the Government has guaranteed his sales ; but it takes an intelligent entrepreneur—and one with some real spirit of enterprise—to grasp the opportunity of receiving technical advice. For these reasons, we regard the provision of technical advice as both a desirable and a legitimate function of a government-sponsored agency.

The arrangement for providing technical advice and assistance to small firms are as follows. First, the Central Small Industries Organisation, through its Service Institutes and Extension Centres, provides a staff of technically qualified people whose job it is to give advice to small entrepreneurs on the technical problems facing them. In order to give demonstrations of technical processes to small entrepreneurs, the CSIO has equipped most of its Service Institutes with common facility workshops. It also sends out demonstration vans into rural areas. A second type of technical assistance is given by the common facility workshops, in undertaking difficult production operations on behalf of small firms at a cost, which (at present), generally, excludes interest and depreciation on the machinery employed. Thirdly, there are the "prototype-cum-production" centres. The object of these is to develop prototypes of machine tools suitable for use in small-scale Indian enterprises, to manufacture them, and to offer to give the blueprints to any small manufacturer who wishes to have them. We shall comment briefly on each of these programmes.

(a) Extension Work

The objects of extension work are wholly admirable ; the main difficulties arise in carrying it out. The greatest of these is the difficulty of finding suitably qualified staff and of persuading them to work for a Government agency, in which they are likely to be worse paid than in a private firm. It is our impression that the present staff of the Small Industries Service Institutes are trying their best to cope with their problems but that they are unable to give sufficiently good advice in many cases. The danger of this situation is that industrialists will lose faith in the Government organisation and fail to use it even where it can be helpful. A possible solution would be to give up the attempt to provide advice on all problems from within the organisation and to direct the staff mainly towards collecting accurate information about the nature of each problem. A staff of "generalists" could then feed problems to experts, who would consist largely of private engineers drawn from a panel. The experts would be paid separately for each job performed and, since specialised advice of this sort would be both more valuable to the entrepreneur and more costly to the Government, it would be desirable to charge the entrepreneur a proportion of its cost. This would serve both to help finance the scheme and to weed out inquiries which were not serious. In any case, services that are paid for (at least in part), are generally more fully appreciated.

One of the fundamental difficulties about giving technical advice to small firms is to keep clearly in mind the purposes for which such advice is being given. Since most small firms work in hopelessly "inefficient" conditions—with old tools, inferior raw materials, and inadequate control of quality—the first reaction of a trained technician is generally to suggest a complete rebuilding of the factory, the purchase of reliable machines and so on. Yet such proposals, if carried out, would convert a small workshop with a low capital-labour ratio into a modern small factory with a high capital-labour ratio. It may be that this is the "right" thing to do—in the sense that the output-capital ratio will be higher after the conversion than before—but this is not certain. A very difficult choice presents itself: Should the technical advice be directed, primarily, towards preserving the low capital-intensity of small firms by making them more efficient in the use of their *existing* resources? Or should the advice aim at converting technically "backward" firms into modern firms using up-to-date machinery and processes, producing a reliable, quality-controlled, modern product? The latter course may be the only sensible one if the firm is to expand and become more efficient in the future; but the former course would save scarce resources of capital now. The problem needs further study, preferably by a combined group of economists and engineers. Whatever the outcome of such a study, however, we believe that in the training of technicians to work in industrial extension work in India, emphasis should be placed on the development of capital-saving methods of production.

This problem is especially relevant to the "demonstration vans" which are now sent out into villages. These vans con-

tain such advanced and elaborate equipment—by village standards—that they are likely to be mere objects of curiosity to
the villager. The vans appear to be designed not so much to
help the village artisan to do a better job with his existing
equipment—or with a modest addition—as to convert him to
the benefits of modern technique. This aim is both inappro-
priate and unrealistic at this stage ; and the demonstration vans
are probably of little use in their present form.

(b) Common Facility Workshops

The main purpose of the common facility workshops is to
undertake specific manufacturing processes on behalf of small
firms which lack the necessary equipment to do the work themselves. The workshop may be specialised, in the sense that it
undertakes only one type of process—electroplating, foundry,
forging, etc.—or it may be a general-purpose workshop. Most
of these workshops have been set up by the Central Small Industries Organisation, but a few have also been established by the
States themselves. Many of them are located in industrial estates.

The common facility workshops that we have seen have been
installed in large factory sheds on industrial estates and equipped
with substantial quantities of first-rate machinery. Scarcely any
of them are at present working anywhere near capacity, and,
except in the really successful estates—such as Guindy—they
find it very difficult to get work to do. Some of them, therefore, have turned away from their original purpose and are
being used for production or training purposes ; but since these
activities have been taken up more to occupy the idle machines
than to fill a known need, they are not usually very successful.
Our impression is that, in general, rather too much emphasis has
been placed on the importance of providing "common facilities",
especially in the smaller industrial estates where the needs are
at present very limited. Moreover, wherever there is a real
demand for common facilities, it should be possible to persuade
private firms to meet it. The Government is not good at operating small enterprises, especially those that need to be flexible
and adaptable.

There is one type of common facility workshop which seems
to be especially dubious. The example we have in mind is the

surgical instruments centre planned for Bombay. The proposal is that this centre should undertake all the difficult operations involved in producing surgical instruments—the punching of the blanks, hardening and tempering—while the small firms that would be served by it would merely shape up the instruments from the blanks and put the final touches after tempering. This scheme seems to us to be neither one thing nor another. It has neither the virtues of a small enterprise—low capital requirements, flexibility, and so on—nor the virtues of medium-scale operation —assured quality, standardisation, long runs at low cost, and economic marketing. For products like surgical instruments— in which guaranteed quality is of the highest importance—we fail to see the point of promoting small firms. It would surely be better—and no more expensive in terms of capital—to encourage the establishment of one or two medium-sized private firms, with the necessary technical skill and equipment to turn out a high quality product. Such products would not only meet India's home requirements but could also become a valuable export line.

(c) Prototype-cum Production Centres

It is not possible, as yet, to say very much about these centres. The first two were planned to start in Rajkot and Okhla but neither of them is yet working. A large amount of valuable machinery is being imported (over Rs. 20 lakhs for Rajkot and about Rs. 36 lakhs for Okhla), but the outcome is still uncertain. Our impression is that these centres will be of most value if they concentrate on *producing* machine tools and leave the arrangements about copying the prototypes to develop afterwards. In any case, the firms that want to copy the prototypes should be obliged to pay a licensing fee ; and there is no obvious reason why the right to copy should be limited to small firms.

FINANCIAL ASSISTANCE

The chief financial disability of small firms is that they are small. Because they are small and unstable, their profits tend to fluctuate widely, and many of them are unable to plough back enough of their earnings to expand. Again, because they are small, they find it difficult to raise loans : their fixed assets are often not sufficient to provide security for a reasonable medium-term loan, and the instability of their profits deters banks from giving them unsecured loans.

Although it is widely assumed that small businesses have a *right* to receive financial help in one form or another, and that it is the Government's business to provide it, these propositions cannot easily be justified. In a free enterprise system small firms must manage as best they can. Those that make good profits will be able to plough back and expand ; they will also be able—if they want to—to raise loan capital on the strength of their profits, and of the growth in their fixed assets. They are doubly blessed. Firms whose profits are small or uncertain will naturally complain that they are unable to do as well as their successful competitors. But that is a law of the competitive market which believers in and promoters of private enterprise must learn to accept. They cannot have it both ways. Either they have private enterprise, with competition, or they have Government intervention, which may lead to socialism. The worst of both worlds, from the social point of view, would be Government intervention to support the weakest and most inefficient producers.

This being said, there is, nevertheless, a case for improving institutional arrangements so as to give small firms a reasonable chance to contact people who might be willing to help them. The commercial banks, on the whole, find that loans to small business are a tiresome nuisance. But, for the sake of those small men who really have the seeds of progress in them, it may be worth the Government's while to establish institutions which will at least take the trouble to look carefully at each request for a loan. And there are also some simple devices which the Government can promote (although they might equally have been started by private organisations, if they had thought of them) to give credit to small (or large) firms with absolute security. These include hire-purchase, mortgage loans and lock-and-key inventory loans.

In India there are now several channels through which small firms can obtain financial help from the Government. First, there are the State Aid to Industries Acts. These empower State Directors of Industries and their officers to give medium-term loans of limited amount to any small firm which they judge to be worthy. The loans may be secured on assets, or—for small loans—they may be covered only by bonds or sureties. The rates of interest recommended by the Central Government (which provides two-thirds of the finance) are 3 per cent for individuals and $2\frac{1}{2}$ per cent for cooperatives—rates which are only a third or a half of what would have to be paid in the open market.

These provisions are very generous and it is not surprising that the amounts disbursed in this way have been increasing rapidly during the Second Plan. By June 1959 it was estimated that Rs. 7.5 crores had been lent to over 20,000 small units ; and the total for the Second Plan period may amount to Rs. 15 crores. Although these figures are no doubt gratifying, to those who measure the performance of a Plan in terms of the amount of money the Government spends, we must confess to some uneasiness about the liberality with which these loans are now being distributed, and especially to the heavily subsidised rates of interest. Reasonably efficient small firms should not find it burdensome to pay a rate of 6 per cent, and even this is really too low for an economy which is so short of capital as India is. A particular danger which arises from channelling so much financial assistance through the State Governments rather than through independent financial institutions is the opportunities it gives to corruption.

The second source of finance for small firms is the State Finance Corporations. These give medium-term loans (10-12 years) on the security of fixed assets (generally in the form of a first mortgage) up to about half the net value of the assets. The loans are intended primarily for financing fixed capital. The usual rate is $6\frac{1}{2}$ per cent, with a rebate of $\frac{1}{2}$ per cent for timely repayment of instalments of principal and payment of interest. In some of the States, the State Finance Corporation have also been made responsible for handling loans under the State Aid to Industries Act. From the beginning of the Second Plan to the end of June 1959, the State Finance Corporations had lent nearly Rs. 3.4 crores to 395 firms. This would appear to be a useful and businesslike operation.

The third major source of Government-sponsored credit to small firms is the State Bank of India. The State Bank has been given a special responsibility for lending working capital to small firms, and it is steadily increasing the number of its branches so as to make such facilities available to new areas. Most of its loans are secured against raw materials or finished goods, either on the lock-and-key system or against hypothecation. The rate of interest charged is in the region of $4\frac{1}{2}$ per cent, depending on the nature of the security. The State Bank, as we have already mentioned, is also acting as agent for the so-called "pilot" scheme for coordinating the provisions of credit from different sources. The State Bank is doing excellent work and it is to be hoped that it will soon be able to extend its operations to all centres of modern small industry.

The fourth major source of finance is the facility of buying machinery on hire-purchase through the National Small Industries Corporation. The Corporation was set up in 1955, and it started its hire-purchase scheme early in the following year. Small firms can obtain machinery through the Corporation (after getting approval from their State Director of Industries) on payment of 20 per cent of the price as "earnest money". The period of repayment is now standardised at seven years (except in the case of ungraded indigenous machines) and the rate of interest charged is generally 6 per cent. In nearly four years of operation—from early 1956 to the end of September 1959—the Corporation had delivered nearly 3,000 machines valued at Rs. 2.6 crores. In most of the industrial estates we encountered a number of firms which had bought machinery in this way. They were generally pleased with the arrangement, but some firms criticised the Corporation for taking so long to deliver the machines and also for charging a commission of 10 per cent. We sympathise with the first criticism but not with the second.

There is no doubt that the hire-purchase scheme has been one of the most successful schemes to be promoted in recent years ; and it is also thoroughly businesslike. Hire-purchase finance is a simple, self-securing and flexible method of giving financial assistance and we believe that there is scope for its further extension. It would be useful, for example, if any firm could obtain a hire-purchase loan on any machine, irrespective of whether it was bought through the National Small Industries Corporation or not. For this purpose, the State Bank of India could well act as the agent of the Corporation in giving the loan and recovering the instalments. At the present time a small firm cannot get hire-purchase facilities unless it shows that the installation of the new machine is technically and economically justified. This criterion, which is necessary for the sanctioning of imports, is irrelevant to the provision of finance, and should no longer be insisted upon.

The final major source of Government financial assistance is the provision of factory buildings in industrial estates. This source is of great and growing importance, but since we have already considered the industrial estates in the previous section we shall make no further comment here.

Apart from these sources, small enterprises can obtain loans from commercial and cooperative banks. Under a new credit guarantee scheme initiated by the Reserve Bank, these banks will be insured against part of their losses on loans to small firms. The scheme is likely to come into operation sometime in 1960 and it will be interesting to see how much effect it has. In principle, such a scheme is excellent, since it gives a fillip to a desired form of lending, but on an almost entirely commercial basis.

One form of financial assistance which has been used only to a small degree is the provision of equity. The outstanding example is the State of Orissa, which, in a desperate attempt to persuade local people to go into industry, has offered to subscribe up to 90 per cent of the equity. This seems to be a somewhat dangerous policy. Since no small entrepreneur worth his salt is prepared to accept a large Government participation in his *equity*, the people who go in for this scheme are likely to be weak, feckless and—in the outcome—unsuccessful ; and the Government will lose most of its money. The provision of equity in small private business is a matter which must inevitably be left to the owner, and to such of his relatives, friends or partners as he can persuade to participate. The Government will have enough to do looking after its equity in the public sector without trying to keep an eye on the fate of thousands of small private businesses.

In conclusion, one of the most important steps that the Government could take to help small firms financially would be to start paying its own bills promptly. At the present time as much as a year can pass between the delivery of goods to the Government and the settlement of the account. Large private businesses are often almost as slow in paying for goods supplied to them, especially those supplied by small firms. On the other hand, small firms have to pay promptly—or even in advance— if they want to receive raw materials. No wonder small firms complain of being short of working capital. If the Government, at the Centre and in the States, were to make it a rule that all Government debts must be settled within 3 months, and that any payment after that date would incur a surcharge of one per cent per month, this would tone up the whole business system— and the Government itself—and be of particular value to small firms.

MARKETING ASSISTANCE

Small firms frequently suffer from serious disabilities in the marketing of their products. To some degree this is inevitable, since the products of small firms are often unstandardised and of variable quality. But it also arises from the imperfections of the market itself, as a result of which excessive advantages often accrue to branded and advertised commodities, or to the firm which happens to have a good wholesale agent. There is, therefore, a case for Government intervention to try to eliminate some of these imperfections and to give small firms a reasonable chance to sell their products on their merits. The sort of pro- gramme that would be appropriate for this purpose would be one designed to *improve information* and to bring producers and dealers into closer contact with one another. For example, the Government could publish a directory of small firms, which should then be circulated to larger firms (which may in this way be induced to buy components from the smaller firms) and to dealers. Similarly, a directory of wholesalers could be compiled for the benefit of small producers. Thirdly, the Government might organise occasional exhibitions of small firms' products, both in order to inform potential customers, and to give encour- agement to the spirit of emulation amongst small firms them- selves. Fourthly, the Government could provide facilities for market research.

A little work along these lines has been started in India (for example, some of the States have compiled directories of small firms and the Central Small Industries Organisation has a market surveys division) but most of the effort in connection with marketing has gone in a different direction. It is in the marketing field that the conflict between the aims of helping small firms for their own sake and the aim of helping them to overcome unnecessary disabilities is most marked. Supporters of the former view appear to believe that small firms should be given a *guarantee* that their products can be sold. Arising from this line of thought there is a scheme (organised by the National Small Industries Corporation) for giving small firms a preference margin of 15 per cent on Government orders. No information is available about how many sales have actually been made on this basis, but they have probably not been large, since there is naturally a good deal of resistance amongst Government purchasing agencies to operating the scheme. But new proposals are now afoot to *compel* the Government to buy a certain proportion of its supplies from small firms. Another programme, already in operation in a limited way, is the establishment (by the NSIC) of wholesale depots to sell selected small enterprise products under the common brand name "Jansevak". The economics of this venture have not been disclosed but there is almost certainly a large element of subsidy involved. There is every likelihood that the organisation will find itself accumulating large unsold stocks ; and similar results will follow if, as has recently been suggested, retail sales emporia are established for the sale of small enterprise products.

The Working Group, which made proposals for the programme of small industries work to be undertaken during the Third Plan, gave its support to a number of questionable proposals for Government marketing assistance to small firms. Apart from the suggestion that the Government should set itself the target of buying 10 per cent of its requirements from small firms, it also proposed that, in giving contracts to large firms, the Government should give preference to those firms that undertook to buy the largest proportion of the components required to meet the contract from small firms. Similarly, it suggested that when a licence is given for the setting up of a new large unit, permission should be given only for the manufacture of those parts which cannot economically be made by small firms. It is difficult to see how such a programme can be administered in practice. The scope for evasion and corruption would be very large.

Going even further, the Working Group gave strong support to the idea of "common production programmes". The essence of this idea is that the market for a particular product (or group of products) should be divided into two parts—one for large enterprises and the other for small. But on what rational principles can the Government decide the proportions of a particular produce that should be made in large and small firms respectively? It is true that such a policy is now being operated in the cotton textile industry, where capacity in the mills is restricted while handloom production is allowed to increase. But this is a case of two *techniques* ; and there is no real danger of large textile manufacturers trying to masquerade as handloom weavers. But in the case of *modern* industry, where both the technical methods and the product are essentially the same for small, medium or large firms, any attempt to allocate a fixed share of the market to one group of firms would be both arbitrary and extremely difficult to enforce. The consequence might well be that large firms would begin to set up small subsidiaries, while at the same time genuinely efficient small firms, which wanted to expand into the medium range, would be prevented from doing so.

Our conclusion on the subject of marketing assistance to small firms is that the Government should concentrate on measures designed to *perfect the market*, for example, by improving information, encouraging contacts between small and large firms and between small firms and dealers, and helping with the organisation of market surveys; but proposals to give small firms special preferences, susidies, fixed shares of the market or guaranteed sales should be strictly eschewed. Measures of the latter sort may seem superficially to be a splendid way of "helping small firms", but they are more likely to turn out to be an obstacle to the development of an efficient, enterprising and successful indigenous industry.

In practice, of course, the greatest measure of assistance that the Government has given to small firms in India has been to impose sharp restrictions on imports. So long as this situation continues—and the probability is that it will continue for at least the next ten or fifteen years—there will really be no difficulty for efficient (or even inefficient) small firms to sell their products. This consideration alone should be sufficient to deter the advocates of "common production programmes".

TRAINING OF WORKERS

Although there is a great surplus of unskilled workers in India, there is a shortage of skilled workers. The normal way in which such a shortage is overcome is by training workers within existing factories; but when industry is expanding rather fast it may be necessary for the Government to make special arrangements for training skilled workers to meet industry's needs. But, before undertaking special training programmes, it is important for the Government to estimate carefully the probable requirements of skilled workers of various categories and the probable supply arising "spontaneously" from within industry. It is not sensible to set up training establishments simply on the grounds that there is a general shortage of skilled workers, and to hope that somehow the trained workers will find employment.

Unfortunately, it appears that a good deal of the training of workers initiated under the auspices of the small industries programme has been undertaken without looking ahead in this way. In a number of the "production-cum-training centres" which have been established, it has been found that after the workers have completed their training there are no jobs for them to take. This is particularly evident in the case of the centres set up in Kerala to provide training for the educated unemployed, the results of which so far have been largely to produce even-more-highly-educated (or trained) unemployed. In practice, since the authorities do not have the heart to throw trained workers out of the centres at the end of their course without any prospects of employment, they tend to be absorbed by the Government, which either keeps them on in the centre itself—which then virtually ceases to be a training centre and concentrates on production—or sets up a new institution to give the workers employment. In either case efforts are usually made to convert the new enterprise into a cooperative; but since enterprises of this sort are not planned with a view to meeting a known market demand, but simply grow under the impetus of the training programme, they usually turn out to be uneconomic.

It is not by any means certain that schemes for training skilled workers will be of direct benefit to small firms. Small firms do not generally want to employ fully trained workers who would expect to receive a higher wage than small firms are prepared to pay. The typical small firm trains its own workers, just as the large one does, and keeps a hold on its workers by the very fact that they were trained up in that establishment and that their training is incomplete. It remains true, of course, that small firms would often do better work if their employees were better trained. But the most practical way of meeting this need— apart from raising the general standard of education for every-one—would be to set up part-time training schemes for workers to which employers could send their workers, or to which the workers themselves could go in their spare time. Some schemes of this sort are in operation at present, for example, courses in blueprint reading ; but there is scope for many more. In no case, however, should courses of this sort be started without first making contact with the local employers—both large and small —and with the trade unions, to find out whether a demand for such courses exists.

THE SUPPLY OF RAW MATERIALS AND POWER

Under present conditions of a booming home market for manu-factured goods, the main obstacles to the growth of small firms are not technical, financial or commercial, or a shortage of skill-ed labour, but shortages of raw materials and power. These are general shortages which affect firms of all sizes ; but they pro-bably affect small firms more acutely, because small firms have less influence on the authorities which make the allocations. So long as these shortages exist, and so long as they are dealt with by allocations rather than through the price mechanism, there is a case for establishing special channels through which small firms can apply for their quotas, so as to ensure reasonably fair treat-ment as between large and small firms in each industry.

But no one who looks into the present arrangements for allo-cating raw materials and power can be satisfied that the more efficient firms get preference over the less efficient. Inevitably, all sorts of personal and political influences are brought to bear in order to obtain these crucial commodities, and it is a common complaint that some firms which receive allocations of raw materials make an easy living by selling them in the "open" market. In the case of steel—which has been in very short supply—the system is not only arbitrary but extremely inefficient. Each year the Iron and Steel Controller makes an allocation of indigenous steel to the States for distribution amongst small firms. But this "allocation" exists only on paper, and the quantity of steel actually delivered to small firms bears practically no relation to it. For example, while in the years 1957-58 to 1959-60 the "allocation" of steel increased from 52,700 tons to 2,75,500 tons, the quantity *actually made available* declined from 42,823 tons to 13,344 tons.[2] We have met small industrialists in various places who were currently receiving deliveries of steel from their registered stockists on quota certificates issued two years previously. Some were even complaining—in 1960— that the authorities had cancelled all outstanding quotas for 1957.

The result of all this is that most small firms are obliged to rely upon the "open" market for a large proportion of their supplies of raw materials. We are, therefore, tempted to suggest that it is time to reconsider the whole allocation system for raw materials and power, with a view to replacing it by the simple price mechanism. In the case of raw materials this would mean that firms which now buy up to 80 per cent of their supplies in the open market would be obliged to buy the whole lot in this way. The effect of using the price mechanism would be, of course, to raise average raw material and power costs to industry, but it would not reduce total supplies—in fact it might well increase them. Much of the difference between the present official prices and the free market prices could be siphoned off by the Government through the imposition of suitable excises on raw materials and power, or by profits accruing to public enterprises. These sums would then be available to replace other indirect taxes which would otherwise have to be imposed to finance the Plan, so that the final cost of living would not necessarily be any higher. Inevitably, a change of this sort would have other repercussions (for example, on the price of exports) and special measures might need to be taken to deal with some of them. But the advantages to industry generally, and especially to small firms, of scrapping the existing controls and permitting the free

[2] *Small Scale Industries, 1959, A Brief Report*, Small Scale Industries Board, 1960, p. 13.

market to operate would, in our opinion, more than offset the disadvantages.

In the light of the above discussion it is difficult to support proposals (such as those made by the Working Group for the Third Plan) to *reduce* the price of electricity to small firms. There is already a large unsatisfied demand for electricity—even at existing prices—and this is one of the chief reasons why small firms are attracted to industrial estates. Incidentally the Working Group appears to think that it is "unfair" that small firms should pay a higher price per unit than larger users, or that they should be charged the cost of bringing power lines to their premises. Along this line of thought it will always be "unfair" for one producer to have lower costs than another and subsidies will have to be given to make the costs of all firms equal.

ADVICE ON THE STARTING OF NEW FIRMS

The great expansion, in recent years, in the demand for manufactured goods—generated by the Plans—has created wide opportunities for the establishment of new manufacturing businesses in the private sector. Many of the entrepreneurs now trying to find a foothold in industry are ex-merchants, especially importers whose supply of goods has been cut off by the import restrictions. There are also other men of capital (including ex-landlords) who, for one reason or another, are shifting their interests into industry. But one of the difficulties which all these potential manufacturers encounter is the lack of knowledge of the most promising lines in which to invest. In the case of the ex-importers, there is often a tendency to go in for the manufacture of a similar product to that which was previously imported, since valuable established trade contracts can then be put at the service of the new enterprise; but even in these cases it may prove necessary for some adjustment to take place. So far as the mass of small artisans are concerned, there is generally little scope for them to choose a line of production other than that for which they are technically qualified, but they also would benefit from some guidance about the most advantageous products on which to concentrate.

The task of giving advice to entrepreneurs on these matters

is clearly one which should be shouldered by the Government, especially in view of the framework of "planning" within which Indian industry is being developed. In principle, the planning authorities should be able to indicate which products are likely to be most in demand during the next ten or fifteen years and the extent to which these demands will be met by public sector projects or by large-scale private ventures already under way. In the case of large manufacturing units, advice of this sort is given by the Ministry of Commerce and Industry, and a list has recently been published showing in which industries new units will be sanctioned. This is an important step forward, and it is to be hoped that this list will be kept regularly up-to-date, so that no misunderstandings may arise. But, in the small-scale sector no similar list has been published centrally. In Madras there is published a list of industries that "can be considered for starting on a small-scale basis"; and it may be that other States have similar lists. The Central Small Industries Organisation has prepared nearly 200 "Model Schemes" for small units, which are an indirect guide to the types of industry which will be looked on with favour. But in the absence of a central list of approved industries, there is a good deal of confusion about what can be done and what cannot be done. Moreover, such lists as have been issued from time to time give no indication of the time for which they will remain valid, nor do the authorities seem to appreciate the importance of amending the lists quickly, as soon as it is apparent that expansion in any direction is going too fast.

There is, in our opinion, no good reason for maintaining two lists of approved industries—one for large-scale and one for small. Such an arrangement could easily degenerate into a system or "reserved industries". But there should be an officially published, up-to-date and comprehensive list, showing against each product, whether there is room for any new capacity to be installed, and if so how much. It might also be possible to mark those products which, it is thought, can be economically produced on a small scale. But this last should be merely an expression of opinion and should have no bearing on whether a licence for the manufacture of such products would be issued or not. The question of scale is one which should be left to the individual entrepreneur to decide. Official interference in a

S.E.—7

decision of this sort can scarcely ever do any good and will often do a lot of harm.

In order to prepare—and keep up-to-date—such a list there is need for a central clearing house, in which the aggregate demand for each product, the capacity for its production, and the supply of raw materials required for its production are brought into relation with one another, and in which the future trend in each of these variables is forecast. (Clearly, the local availabilities of power and transport for each manufacturing unit should also be taken into account in computing its "capacity".) One of the difficulties in the way of doing this exercise efficiently, at present, is the lack of accurate information about these variables, especially in the case of products which are mainly produced by small firms. There is, therefore, a need to improve the statistical work in this field—in fact, one can almost say to *start* the statistical work in this field. It will not be easy to get small firms into the habit of providing regular statistics about their operations ; but, in the meantime, one immediately useful step would be to collect information centrally about the new capacity sanctioned in each industry by each State. If each State were to report once a month on the new capacities sanctioned for small firms, and these results, after aggregation, were circulated back to the States, it should be possible to avoid some of the unnecessary over-expansion of particular lines which has been witnessed in recent years.

Some of the State authorities—and their associated central small industries officers—have felt it their responsibility not only to give advice to entrepreneurs looking for a suitable line of investment, but also to go out and *recruit* new entrepreneurs from amongst people who are not at present in industry, so as to claim that they have established entirely "new" small-scale enterprises. This is, in part, a reflection of the idea that there are too few small firms in India at the present time and that one of the main functions of the small industries programme is to "create" more small firms. But in part it is also a reflection of an actual shortage of local entrepreneurs in the more backward areas. In these areas we have found entrepreneurs in the industrial estates who were previously local shopkeepers or cultivators, who had been persuaded by the local small industries officers to move into industry. As an inducement to do this,

such people had usually been offered every possible assistance—
a factory shed, machinery on hire-purchase, working capital, allocations of power and raw materials, assistance in recruiting labour
(especially technically trained personnel) and sometimes even a
guaranteed sale for the product. The amount of effort put in by
the officials in order to create one new entrepreneur is sometimes
out of all proportion to their potential usefulness to the community.

CHAPTER V

GENERAL CONCLUSIONS

In India, small manufacturing enterprises fall into two main groups : traditional cottage industries, which are largely rural and serve local markets ; and modern small enterprises, which are largely urban, non-household, and serve wider markets. Traditional industries use traditional techniques, which are essentially labour-using and capital-saving ; modern small factories use modern techniques, which are basically the same as those used by modern large factories.

The principal argument put forward in favour of small enterprises is that they "give employment". This, although true, is irrelevant, since the problem facing India is how to save capital and other scarce resources, not how to use abundant resources (unless the use of the abundant resources helps to save the scarce resources). From the standpoint of saving capital there is much to be said for the traditional village industries—especially where the capital is already in existence ; but the obstacle to making more use of these industries is that, as incomes rise, demand tends to move away from "inferior" traditional products towards modern products. This trend can only be reversed by measures —such as subsidies and differential taxation—which themselves change the relative advantages (from a capital-saving point of view) of traditional and modern industry ; and there is, therefore, a limit to the extent that demand can justifiably be diverted in this way. This limit has probably already been reached in India —and even surpassed in some cases, e. g. khadi.

Within the modern sector of manufacturing industry—with which we are primarily concerned—available evidence suggests that small factories use more capital *and* more labour per unit of output than larger factories. The difference in the output-capital ratios is particularly marked when account is taken of the fact that large factories can more easily be organised on a multi-shift basis than small factories. From the point of view of saving capital, medium or large multi-shift factories give the best results, and small factories usually the worst. There is, therefore, no general case for promoting small modern factories on these grounds.

The second main argument for giving special assistance to small enterprises is that they are a means of decentralising industry. Here again there is a confusion between village industries, which are in their nature decentralised, and small modern factories, which require an urban environment in order to flourish. The revival of village industries would encourage decentralisation, but is largely precluded by the considerations mentioned above. Small modern factories cannot be forced out into rural areas, where the necessary facilities of trade, communications and finance are lacking, and where enterprise and skilled labour are scarce. The decentralisation of modern industry can proceed in the first instance only so far as the larger or medium-sized towns, or to special locations where local sources of raw materials are available. The pioneers in this movement should be the larger enterprises—whether public or private—which can master their new environment and establish the facilities they require. Smaller firms will follow when a favourable environment for their development has been created.

Another group of arguments for promoting small enterprises derives from social and political considerations. Some of these appear, on analysis, to be based on misconceptions; others are value judgements, with which we do not find ourselves particularly in sympathy. In any case, we believe that it would be a mistake to follow a policy of promoting small enterprises for purely political reasons, if the economic arguments are clearly against this course.

The last, and most important, argument for promoting small firms is that there is a shortage of entrepreneurial talent for running medium or large-scale enterprises and that this can be offset by increasing the number of small firms. It is true that there is an abundant supply of small entrepreneurs in India and that there is a shortage of medium-sized factories. But this is hardly an argument for *increasing* the share of small firms in manufacturing—which the statistics show is already larger in India than in several other countries, including Japan—but rather for helping existing small firms to improve their methods so as to *grow* into larger and more efficient organisations. In this way, especially, the share of medium-sized factories in total output can be augmented.

The conclusion, from these arguments, is that the policy for small modern enterprises in India should not be directed—as it tends to be at present—towards the creation of more small units *for their own sake*, but towards a general improvement in the efficiency of existing enterprises and the creation of opportunities for *enterprising* new firms to be successful and to grow. The emphasis of small industry policy should be switched away from the giving of preferences, subsidies and special measures of protection to small firms, towards measures which *remove disabilities* of small firms and give them a fair chance to compete in the market.

In the light of these considerations, we have examined the existing programmes for assisting modern small enterprises, with special attention to the industrial estates programme. Our main conclusions on industrial estates serve to confirm the conclusions reached about modern small factories in general. Factories in industrial estates do not have a particularly advantageous output-capital ratio ; indeed, up to the present they have shown even more unsatisfactory results than might have been expected. One of the main reasons for this is that most of the estates have been built on too costly a scale. In addition, many of the factories are still unoccupied; others, which are occupied, are not yet working, and even amongst those that are working only a few are making full use of the facilities provided. As a result, the amount of employment given by the estates so far is disappointingly small. If steps are taken to economise on construction costs of future estates, and to fill up the factories with promising concerns as soon as they are completed, the amount of employment given by the end of the Third Plan may achieve a significant level.

Industrial estates so far erected in backward areas have not proved a success. Future location policy should take full account of the importance to the small firm of having good local facilities, including raw material dealers, wholesale agents, financial institutions, and so forth. To some extent, backward areas may be able to obtain entrepreneurs by migration from other parts of India ; but, in general, backward areas can only be industrialised if large and medium-sized enterprises lead the way. The siting of estates, within towns, should also be guided more by economic and technical considerations—with due regard to the needs of the firms entering the estates—and less by a system of priorities which results in the estates being sited on land that is of little or no value to anyone else.

Industrial estates should be regarded not as homes for the weak and the inefficient but as nursery beds of small enterprise. It should be taken for granted that most firms entering industrial estates will grow, so that in due course they will become too big for the estate. Hence, it is desirable to provide facilities in a nearby industrial area for these "graduate" firms to build their own factories, with suitable financial assistance. We do not consider that the firms now in industrial estates should be allowed to purchase their sheds—either on hire-purchase or in any other way. Nor should they be allowed to make radical alterations to the building. The aim of the estates should be to provide for a steady turnover of tenants so as to give the most benefit to those who are most in need of it.

In our review of the other programmes of assistance to small enterprises we have noted many good features—especially the attention being given to providing technical advice and financial assistance—but also some tendencies to resort unnecessarily to subsidies, protection and other devices designed to give small firms special preferences. Fortunately, the most objectionable of these devices—the so-called "common production programme", which involves the allocation of specified shares of the market to large and small firms respectively—has not yet gone much beyond the point of being discussed (except for two industries) in the modern manufacturing sector.

In relation to technical advice—which we believe to be a most important part of the programme—we suggest that higher standards can be attained if Government technical officers are mainly "generalists", who can call in the services of part-time specialists from private and public industry when required. For specialised advice, however, small firms should be charged at least half of the cost.

In the financial field we should like to see a further extension of the network of State Bank branches and the wider availability of hire-purchase facilities (for plant and machinery). We are critical of the very low rates of interest charged on loans given under the State Aid to Industries Acts and also of direct Government investment in the equity of small firms.

Marketing assistance should, in our opinion, be limited to measures designed to spread information and perfect the market. Preference margins for Government purchases from small firms, reserved shares of the market, guaranteed sales, and Government-sponsored internal trade organisations for the sale of small enterprise products seem to us to be less likely to stimulate enterprise than to spread stagnation by the elimination of the spur of competition.

Amongst other detailed suggestions for the improvement of the small industries programme, we have proposed that serious consideration be given to the abolition of the present system of allocation of raw materials, and its replacement by a free market. The sytem of allocating raw materials is a system of distributing valuable privileges which encourages corruption. But even an incorruptible authority would find it impossible to make rational allocations amongst thousands of small firms. Many small firms make no attempt to obtain an allocation of raw materials, and even those that receive one do not get the corresponding raw materials. The "open" market is already the major source of supplies for many—if not most—small firms ; and it would be better to apply the same rule to everyone. Appropriate adjustments to taxation would have to accompany any such move.

The major lesson that can be drawn from this study is the importance of concentrating on the promotion of *efficiency* and *growth*, rather than on the creation of new small firms for their own sake. We believe that there is an important role for small enterprises to play in Indian economic development, but that the main encouragement should be given to the most efficient and promising small firms and that all must learn to stand on their own feet.

INDEX

INDEX

Note : The following abbreviations are used :

def = defined;
desc = described;
irt = in relation to;
qirt = quoted in relation to;
rirt = referred in relation to.

91